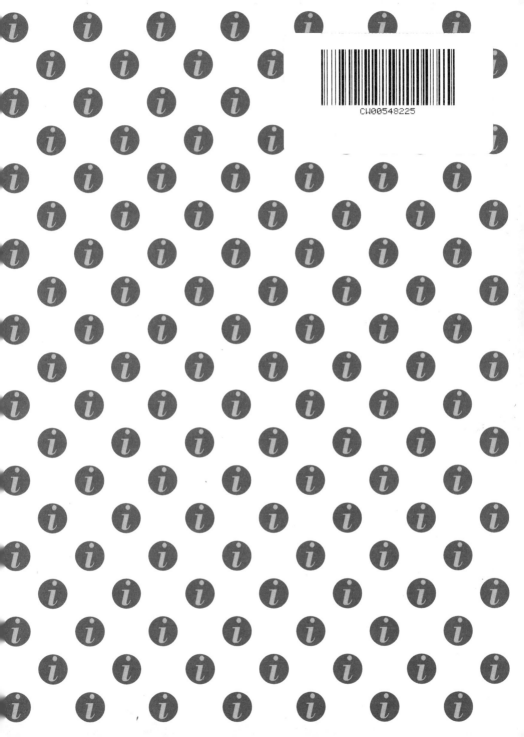

CW00548225

IDENTIFYING

i

POCKET KNIVES

The new compact study guide and identifier

POCKET KNIVES

The new compact study guide and identifier

BERNARD LEVINE

CHARTWELL
BOOKS, INC.

A QUINTET BOOK

Published by Chartwell Books
A Division of Book Sales, Inc.
114, Northfield Avenue
Edison, New Jersey 08837

This edition produced for sale in the U.S.A., its
territories and dependencies only.

ISBN 0-7858-1026-9

This book was designed and produced by
Quintet Publishing Limited
6 Blundell Street
London N7 9BH

Creative Director: Richard Dewing
Art Director: Clare Reynolds
Designer: Peter Laws
Editor: Jane Hurd-Cosgrave
Project Editor: Debra Sellman

The material used in this publication previously appeared in Pocketknives by Bernard Levine.

We would like to thank the following for the help with the photographs in this book:
The members of the Mason-Dixon Knife Club; Simon Moore; Barrett-Smythe Limited; The
Forschner Group; Dr H. Melnick; Victorinox Cutlery Limited; Jim Hughes; Remington; Imperial
Schrade Corporation; Bernard Levine; Weyer International of Toledo; National Knife
Collectors Association; Robert Wentz; The American Military Edged Weaponry Museum.

The circa 1910 drawings in the chapter "How Pocket Knives were Made" were previously
reproduced in The Romance of Knife Collecting, 4th Ed. by Mrs L. Ferguson, published in
1976 and long out of print. They were reproduced in Knife World magazine. Used by
permission.

Typeset in Great Britain by
Central Southern Typesetters, Eastbourne
Manufactured in Singapore by Eray Scan Pte Ltd
Printed in Singapore by Star Standard Industries Pte Ltd

CONTENTS

Identifier

INTRODUCTION

POCKETKNIVES at first glance seem such an everyday item, it is a wonder why so many people collect them. Yet it is precisely their familiar charm and infinite variety that gives them their appeal. A pocketknife is a companion for years, even for life. As the tool-using creatures *par excellence*, we are always sure to have our trusty pocketknife with us! But a pocketknife is more than merely a tool—it is also a mechanical device (and occasionally a very complex one), and a work of great craft and technology— even an elaborate work of art.

To the affluent and sophisticated, fine pocketknives are like personal jewelry, and

Left *Roman folding knife handle (base missing) depicting an embracing couple in bronze. The way her robe is slipping off suggests a Gallo-Roman design 3rd to 4th century AD.*

collecting them has been an enjoyable habit for many centuries. In 1862, Abraham Lincoln was presented with a handsome, five-blade knife, which recently sold at an auction for nearly $100,000. Today, there are many exclusive shops around the world (such as the world-famous Barrett-Smythe Galleries in New York; Hawthorn Galleries in Branson, Missouri; the S.F. Gun Exchange in San Francisco; OK-YESS Knives in Tokyo; Messer Hendel in Braunschweig, Germany; Messer Klötzli in Burgdorf, Switzerland; G. Lorenzi in Milan; E. Lorenzi in Vienna, Austria; and M. Kindal in Paris) that sell exquisite, contemporary, handcrafted folding knives, some of them engraved by the world's leading engravers, at prices that range from several hundred dollars up to $50,000 each—quite a sum for an "everyday" item!

Beyond these technical, esthetic, and status considerations, a pocketknife of any age (even a brand-new one) is an historical artifact that was made in a particular time and place, by particular people, and for a particular market. Because pocketknives are universal items that have been around since ancient times, their various forms, usages, styles, and brands have proliferated beyond imagining—efforts to document and classify them have occasionally approached the complexity of a paleontologist's work in

Above *Case XX Made in USA 5-dot (1975) premium penknife, red-bone handles.*

identifying the taxonomy of fossils! Less than half of the 5,000 or so known pocketknife brands have been documented, and old brands are being rediscovered every day. Most of these brands represent between two dozen and two thousand distinct patterns—even more, if the particular brand spanned several generations, or was distributed worldwide.

This book is intended as a basic introduction to pocketknives, and as such assumes no foreknowledge on the part of the reader. Nevertheless, it contains a wealth of information that will prove valuable and revealing to the most advanced collector or knife dealer, and even to manufacturers who have spent a lifetime in the cutlery industry. However, it has been written specifically for the collector or enthusiastic pocketknife fan, to explain why certain knives are interesting and collectible, and therefore valuable. With study and experience, including the information contained in this book, you can learn to read these artifacts as precisely as an archeologist reads potsherds, and thus enhance your enjoyment of pocketknife collecting, whether as a hobby, or for more commercial purposes.

THE ORIGIN AND EVOLUTION OF POCKETKNIVES

THE STORY OF pocketknives prior to the 18th century is part conjectural, part archeological. Excavations have revealed figural folding knives that date from the later years of the Roman Empire, which means that they were not exactly "pocket" knives, since sewn-on pockets had not yet been invented. Ancient and medieval folding knives made up for their technical deficiencies with an abundance of exuberant decoration.

Those earliest-known folding knives had no backsprings in their handles. The job of a pocketknife's spring is to apply tension to the blade and to keep it in place, when both are open and closed. Without a spring, friction alone must be relied upon to keep a folding blade from flopping around. To this day, inexpensive folding knives are made in the ancient Roman style—without backsprings. These are known as "penny knives," because until recent years, the

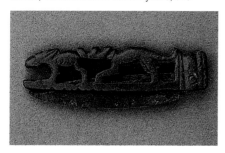

Above *Roman folding knife, the bronze openwork is half cast in the form of a hound catching a rabbit. 2nd–4th century, AD.*

plainest versions of such knives sold for a penny a piece.

Although the idea of the spring-back knife seems to be older, reliable spring steel was a product of the mid-18th century—1742, to be precise. It was the invention of Benjamin Huntsman, a clock maker in Sheffield, England. Sheffield's cutlers soon learned to use Huntsman's crucible-cast steel for both the blades and the springs of their finer cutlery items, and on this new metal was the city's world preeminence as a cutlery center based.

The generation after Huntsman's invention witnessed remarkable advances in cutlery design and technology, especially in Paris, France, where cheap, mass, factory-produced pocketknives—or "penny knives"—was a notable 18th-century development. Much of the basic design and technology of modern cutlery was created there at that time, largely by master cutler Jean-Jacques Perret. Perret set down a detailed record of his work in *The Art of the Cutler*, published in 1771; more than a century later, "inventors" in America, England, and Germany were still receiving patents for cutlery mechanisms that had been copied line for line from Perret's book.

Despite the advent of factory mass-production, well into the middle of the 19th century, all of the high-quality folding knives were still made by hand. These were produced by skilled craftsmen, primarily in England, France, Germany, Italy, and Bohemia, and therefore had a seemingly endless variety of patterns and styles. To

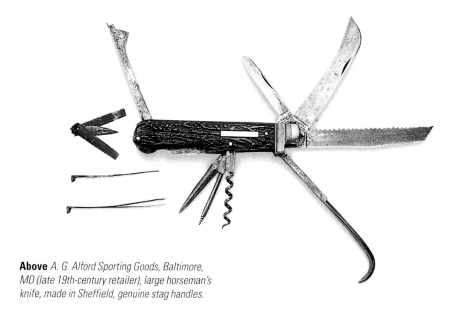

Above *A. G. Alford Sporting Goods, Baltimore, MD (late 19th-century retailer), large horseman's knife, made in Sheffield, genuine stag handles.*

collectors, perhaps the most remarkable knives of that period were the folding sidearms. Ornate and usually large, these folding dirks, bowie knives, and folding-knife-pistol combinations were made in infinite variation in England and other Western European countries from the 1830s into the early 20th century, both for domestic sales and for export to America. However, as mass markets began to develop, especially in the Western hemisphere, standardization of pocketknife patterns for sale in those markets gradually advanced.

Beginning in the 1840s, emigrant cutlers from Europe began to develop a pocket cutlery industry in the United States. In America, where land and resources were plentiful, but skilled labor was scarce, cutlery manufacturers pioneered machine methods and simplified processes—another force favoring standardized patterns.

Innovative men like Samuel Mason and C. W. Platts, Homer Twitchell, Matthew Chapman, and Joseph Gardner, most of them Sheffield-trained prior to 1860, laid down the technological foundations of the burgeoning American cutlery industry. Meanwhile, traditional handcrafted methods remained near-universal in Sheffield through the 1890s, and continue today on a limited scale.

From the 1880s up to 1940, pocketknives evolved primarily through marketing and design. Technology was remarkably stable in that period, which is viewed by collectors today as the "Golden Age" of pocket cutlery. The most important cutlery innovation of that period—the invention of stainless steel in 1914 (simultaneously by Elwood Hayes of Indiana and Harry Brearley of Sheffield) —revolutionized table cutlery, but had no effect on the pocket cutlery industry until after 1950.

TYPES OF POCKETKNIVES

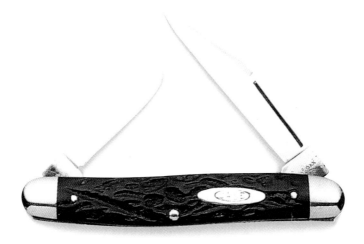

Above *Case Tested double-end premium jack, with "rough-black" composition handles.*

ALL POCKETKNIVES can be divided into three basic types, on the basis of structure. Functionally, by contrast, there are dozens of different types of folding knife. The three structural types are jackknives, penknives, and multiblades.

Like the taxonomy of plants and animals, the taxonomy of pocketknives has its share of ambiguity, fuzzy boundaries, and polite disagreement among experts. Still, all folding knives can reasonably be assigned to one of these three types.

Jackknives and Penknives

"Jackknives" are stout and simply made. As a rule, a jackknife has its blade or blades (often two, very rarely three) in one end of the handle.

"Penknives," as a rule, are delicate and finely made. They have their blades— generally two to four, occasionally more—in both ends. Some penknives include a nail-file manicure blade.

Just to make life interesting, there are exceptions to both of these rules. Stout knives with a large blade in each end are called "double-end jackknives." Very small knives with a single, tiny blade in one end are the original "penknives," designed for sharpening quill pens. To avoid confusion, collectors now call these "quill knives." In addition to ordinary penknives and quill knives, the "penknife" designation also embraces two distinctive sub-types. These are called "whittlers" (a modern collector name) and "lobsters" (a traditional cutlery-industry name).

• Whittlers
A basic whittler is a three-blade knife. It has two backsprings that are separated at one end, but abut each other at the opposite end. A stout, master blade is mounted at

Right *Remington swell-center whittler, pearl handle. Wharncliffe whittler (mark obscure), bone handles.*

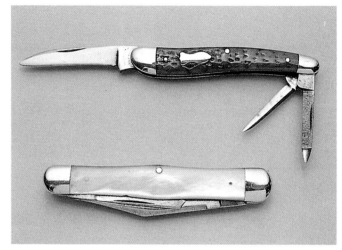

Below *"Case Brothers" (Case Classic) 1990 limited-edition sleeveboard whittler, genuine stag (contract-made by Queen).*

Bottom *A Ka-Bar limited-edition, lockback English jack with folding guard, stag-bone handles, and dog-head shield, lies* *above the James Ward & Co., rare American-made folding dirk with folding guard, horn handles, c 1860s.*

the end where the two springs touch, which is as thick as both the springs together. Two shorter and thinner blades, one on each of the springs, are mounted at the other end. This particular combination of blades makes larger "whittlers" well suited for whittling. However, the same construction was also used on smaller, more delicate, three-blade penknives, which are also called "whittlers" by collectors.

While most pocketknife manufacture has been substantially automated today,

• JACKKNIVES •

Notes: (FH = large version used as folding hunter die) (DE = also used as a double-end jackknife die) • Equal-End Jack (DE) Sunfish (Elephant Toenail) (DE only) • Slim Equal-End Jack • Regular Jack Electrician's Knife, Barlow Knife, Boy's Knife, No. 2 Scout Knife, English Jack (FH), Stabber pattern • Slim Jack (Slim Regular Jack) Melon Tester, Physician's Knife • Curved Regular Jack (FH) Rope Knife • Sleeveboard Jack US WWI Electrician's Knife • Jumbo Jack (large Sleeveboard) (DE) • Curved Jack (the traditional English farmer's knife) Pruning Knife, Maize (grain sorghum) Knife, Cotton Sampler, Rope Knife, Whaler • Swayback Jack • Congress Jack • Crown Jack (also called "Coffin Jack") • Swell-End Jack ("Tear Drop") • Swell-Center Jack ("Coke Bottle") (FH) • Balloon Jack (DE) Platt's Sunfish (DE only) • Swell-Center Regular Jack (FH) Trapper, Large Trapper • Gunstock Jack Gunstock Budding Knife • Premium Jack (DE) Premium Trapper (DE) • Gunstock Premium Jack • Serpentine Jack Peanut, Wharncliffe Jack (DE) • Slim Serpentine Jack Light Trapper • Eureka Jack (Swell-Center Serpentine Balloon Jack) (DE) • Canoe (DE) • Surveyor (Swell-Center Canoe) (DE) • Fishtail Jack • Fish Jack • Tickler (Powder Horn) Fish Knife • Clasp type (FH only) •

• PENKNIVES •

Note: (WH = also used as whittler die) Senator Pen (Equal-End) (WH) • Sleeveboard Pen (WH) Jumbo (WH only), Physician's (WH) • Oval Pen (also called "Cigar," "Anglo-Saxon Knife") (WH) • "Gunstock" Pen • Congress Pattern (WH) Tobacco Knife • Crown Pen (also called "Coffin Pen") (WH) • "Modern Crown" Pen • Swell-Center Pen (including Balloon Pen) (WH) Jenny Lind • Premium Serpentine Pen • Wharncliffe Pattern (WH) • "Dog-leg" Serpentine Pen (WH) • Swell-Center Serpentine Pen (WH) Norfolk Pattern (WH only) • Swell-Center Congress Knife (Sway-Back Pen) (WH) •

whittler construction still requires a lot of skilled handwork, and the pattern is now virtually extinct, except by a few handmakers or in expensive, German-made, limited editions.

The earliest whittler-type knives, made in 18th-century Paris, had a single spring split down the middle of most of the length, but using two springs proved both easier and stronger. In some whittlers, a tapered center liner divides the two springs for most of their length. In others, a stubby "catch bit"

Top *W. R. Case & Sons "opal pearl," Sheffield-pattern lobster.*

Bottom *Victorinox "Classic," equal-end lobster penknife.*

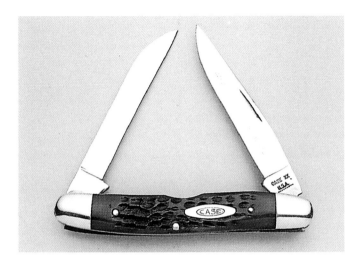

Left *Case XX USA 1971 "Hawbaker's Special," improved muskrat, red stag-bone handles.*

Below *Miller Bros Cutlery, Meriden, CI, swell-center hunting knife, ebony. The use of tiny screws to retain the handles was a registered trademark of Miller Bros.*

divides only the two small blades from each other. A knife with *three* blades and *three* springs is definitely not a whittler, although some Sheffield cutlers made five-blade whittlers, which are rare and very valuable.

• Lobsters

A "lobster" is a penknife with blades at both top and bottom, and with its springs concealed inside the center of the handle. Lobsters are fragile and elegant. Before World War II, they were among the most costly of pocketknives, but today most collectors prefer larger knives that make a more impressive display.

• Folding Hunters

Today's knife collectors favor big folding knives, especially the hunting knives. Folding hunters are generally $4\frac{1}{2}$ to $5\frac{1}{2}$ inches long when closed. They have one or two large blades, and are a type of jackknife.

Classic folding hunters were made on a variety of standard handle dies (*see* page 18): the swell-center or "Coke bottle," the swell-center regular or "Trapper style," and four or

Above *Case XX folding hunter, red stag-bone.*

13

Top *Imperial five-blade, official Boy Scout (USA) knife, Delrin plastic handles.*

Above *Camillus easy-open regular jack with jigged-bone handles and steel mounts, made for the US Army in World War II.*

five variations on the curved clasp-knife. Many firms still make clasp-type folding hunters, but their popularity has declined substantially since the 1960s.

Virtually all modern-style folding hunters, with their curved grip and stout metal frame, were either copied or derived from a single innovative prototype—the original Buck Model 110 folding hunter, introduced in 1962. Buck now makes many variations on its original design, and the 110 itself has seen quite an evolution of form and technology. Today, there is hardly a single pocketknife factory or handcraftsman of folding knives who does not make knives that are based at least in part on Buck's revolutionary 1962 design.

Multiblades

The category "multiblade" includes all knives with three or more blades, of which one or more are gadget-type blades, such as can or bottle openers, leather punchers, corkscrews, forks, and spoons. It also includes stout knives with three or more cutting blades, and a special-purpose blade(s), generally called "cattle knives" and "premium stock knives" (cattle-knife handle dies have names, since most of them are built on the same frames as double-end jackknives). Other multiblade shapes are either very unusual or are grouped into scout-utility knives, horseman's knives, sportsman's knives, cattle knives, stock knives, plier and wrench knives (including miner's dynamite knives), and fork-knife-spoon combinations.

Scout-Utility and Soldier's Knives

Perhaps the most familiar American multiblade is the scout-utility knife. This has four blades (rarely, three, five, or six), in

Right *Unmarked Central European take-apart multi-blade combination knife, ivory handles.*

Below *Latima, Italy, pocket-watch/knife, stainless steel handles.*

Below *Case XX M4045 utility knife with metal handles, British-style can-opener blade.*

the same equal-end handle as the standard cattle knife, from which (along with the European-style sportsman's knife) it was derived. There are over 30 different, official Boy Scout knives, more than a dozen official Girl Scout knives, and at least five official Campfire Girls' knives in this pattern, but hundreds more commercial variants.

Millions of American Scouts and ordinary consumers have used these knives since their introduction *circa* 1910; millions more US soldiers and marines have used them since the US Army adopted this pattern in 1941. British and Commonwealth

Left *Unmarked Central European horseman's combination knife, genuine stag handles. Blades: clip master blade, pen blade, combination saw can-opener, scissors, hoof-pick with attached carriage key, hollow leather punch, and corkscrew.*

scout and military folding knives, on the other hand, derived from 18th-century sailor's jackknives, but now have many similar features to their American counterparts.

US sailors used British-style sailor's jackknives until World War I, when a smaller, American version was adopted. In World War II, the US Navy switched to fixed, bladed knives, except for medical staff, who used utility knives, and lifeboat stores, which used folding rope knives. Allied special operations units during World War II commissioned a wide variety of knives for secret missions from both US and British cutlery firms. Most were unmarked and had fixed blades, but some, including a distinctive, all-metal, pliers-type multiblade, similar to a miner's dynamite knife, but incorporating a can-opener and three hacksaw blades, were folding knives.

• Sportsman's Knives

Sportsman's knives are elaborate multiblades with a multitude of specialized blades. Today's most familiar sportsman's knives are the "Swiss Army" knives, made both by Elsener/Victorinox of Ibach and by Wenger of Delemont—and imitated by scores of firms worldwide. Today, "Swiss Army" knives are made in dozens of different models, but in earlier times, there was much more variety of this knife type—in their size, shape, blade type, and sheer complexity. Some late 18th- and early 19th-century horseman's knives (the name for sportsman's knives with a folding hoof-pick on the back) even had blades folding up inside other blades.

Today, red plastic is the handle material on these knives. In the old days, genuine stag was standard, but metal, bone, horn, ivory, tortoise-shell, and pearl were options.

...

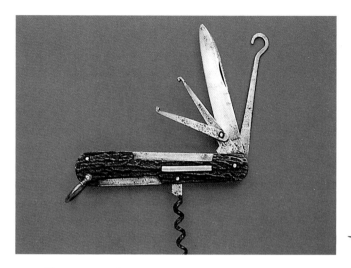

Left *H. G. Long & Co., Sheffield, sportsman's combination knife with genuine stag handles. Blades: patent, adjustable, shotshell extractor, spear-master blade, large buttoner for gaiters, and corkscrew.*

Handle Dies and Named Patterns

The sheet-metal frame pieces (called "liners") of a pocketknife handle were stamped with a set of steel dies, and each different shape came to be called a "handle die." Every jackknife and penknife handle die has a name. Those we use today are the result of a standardization of patterns that developed between 1840 and 1890. The handle dies before that period probably had names also, but most of them seem to have been lost.

The term "handle die" refers to the shape of a pocketknife's handle. "Pattern" is even more specific, indicating a particular combination of handle die and blades. In a cutlery catalog, a particular pattern number specifies the handle die, size, blades, mount materials, and handle material.

The standard handle-die names of the period *circa* 1865–1965 are listed on page 12. After each handle-die name are the named patterns built on these dies. Some are no longer made; most modern shapes since that time haven't yet been given names.

Above
Digby's, Kelham Island (Sheffield), contemporary deluxe presentation knife, pearl, engraving, filework.

• British Pocketknife Patterns
While much of Sheffield's output went to American and Commonwealth markets, the city's single most important cutlery market was Britain itself, especially after 1891. Every pocketknife firm in Sheffield selected "town patterns," pocketknife patterns typical of Sheffield that were sold there.

The best-known town pattern was the horseman's multiblade. At its most basic, this pattern includes a spear blade, pen

17

Below *German-style folding bowie, "Le Louis d'Or" (gold-coin brand) made in France, stag handles.*

blade, and saw on top, with a corkscrew, augur, punch, and combined hoof-pick-nutcracker on the bottom. Other town patterns included the senator and congress penknives (originally developed for the American trade), the sailor's knife used by the military, the "church window," and the curved jackknife with sheepfoot blade favored by farmers in the Channel Islands, Orkneys, Dover, and Donegal.

The English version of the folding hunting knife (so typical that Americans called it the "English jack") was a simple, regular or sleeveboard pattern, 4 to 7 inches long when closed, with a single locking clip or spear-point blade. The favorite lobster pattern in Britain (called the "Sheffield-pattern lobster" in the US) was a bolstered sleeveboard with an extra-wide manicure blade set into the back. As late as 1970, Wostenholm's was making large quantities of Sheffield-pattern lobsters to be sold by Cartier, the well-known jeweler.

• French Pocketknife Patterns

France boasts an ancient cutlery industry, and a wide array of traditional pocketknife patterns. Best known today are the Opinels from Cognin. Standard Opinels, sold worldwide, are wood-handled penny knives with a rotating-ferrule lock. Deluxe horn- and ivory-handled models made for collectors are sold by Courty et Fils in Paris.

Almost as familiar is the Laguiole, a

locking-clasp knife with a slender, yatagan-style blade, and often with a corkscrew in the back. Pierre Calmels makes the genuine article in the town of Laguiole, where his grandfather created the pattern, but the best-known, exported Laguioles come from G. David.

The French pradel, named after a 19th-century family of Thiers cutlers, is strikingly similar to the most basic American jackknife, the Barlow, named after a 17th-century family of Sheffield cutlers. "Pradel" is the name for a barehead, regular jack with a single, short-pull spear blade, and also the French name for this blade.

The Mediterranean island of Corsica, which is French territory, boasts its own, distinctive style of "Vendetta Corse" folding knives. These self-guard clasp knives with long bolsters have deadly, needle-sharp blades. They are made in a wide range of sizes, both in Thiers and on Corsica.

• German Pocketknife Patterns

For a whole millennium, German cutlers were the swordsmiths of the world, and for more than a century, they were the pocket cutlers of the world as well. Endless varieties of pocketknives were made in Solingen for export, with a more limited variety made for German domestic sale.

The most typical German pocketknives are the large, stag-handled, folding hunters. These were made in many sizes and shapes,

Left *Hoffritz (US retailer) German-made folding pruning knife with pruning blade, pruning shears, and pruning saw, with wood handles.*

Right *Stainless-steel (Japan), equal-end lobster penknife with stainless-steel handles. Blades: spear-master blade, scissors, manicure blade, and folding cigarette lighter.*

and with auxiliary blades—usually a saw and a corkscrew. Also typical was the clasp knife with a horn or stag or deer-foot handle (the latter complete with fur and hoof), which was the ancestor of the American pattern called the "tickler" or "toothpick." An inexpensive, all-metal version of this knife, made by Kauffmann, has been popular in Germany since World War I.

• Traditional Japanese Pocketknife Patterns

Today, most of the pocketknives made in Japan are copied from American or European prototypes, but Japan does have its own traditional style of folding knife. This all-metal Higonokami knife boasts a laminated-steel blade with a cut-off point and super-sharp cutting edge. The blade is saber ground on the front and flat on the back. High-quality examples are signed with a calligraphic flourish, both on the flat of the blade and on the steel handle.

19

HOW POCKETKNIVES
WERE MADE

THE DRAWINGS OPPOSITE (from an E. C. Simmons Hardware Co. catalog, *circa* 1910) show how a typical, equal-end jackknife of the time was made. The first step was to forge the blades from a carbon-steel strip (Nos. 1 and 2), usually a punch-press operation (as in America), or done by hand (as in Sheffield). The forged blades were then die cut to shape and heat treated, after which the tangs were drilled, the surfaces ground, and the flats of the tang filed (Nos. 3 and 4). Springs were produced in much the same way as blades, except they were not forged before being die cut (Nos. 5–7). The parts for the frame were made with chunks of nickel silver or mild steel. These were die cut from thick stock, and then stamped or "coined" to form the bolsters, usually with a stud projecting from the inner surface (Nos. 9–11). Properly spaced holes were then drilled in strips of brass, with pairs of bolsters "chopped on" to these (Nos. 12 and 13). Then the strips were cut with "pattern dies" to make the final shape of the knife's handle (No. 14). The resulting frame piece was called a "scale."

Meanwhile, the "handle covers" were prepared from wood, bone, ivory, pearly, stag, or a synthetic material (No. 15), and then fitted to the scales, with the front cover being inletted to fit the shield (Nos. 16 and 17). Holes were drilled for rivets, and also one in each bolster, one in each end of the cover, two in the shield (No. 18), and one in the bottom center to anchor the spring. The handle rivets and shield rivets were then set, and the knife was assembled (No. 20) and given to a cutler, who did the final adjusting to ensure "walk and talk," the smooth operation and positive snap when opened and closed. Lastly, the blades were given a final polish, then honed and etched (No. 21), before the finished knives could be oiled, wrapped, and sold.

Factors and Factories

Originally, the word "factory" meant the warehouse of a factor. A factor was primarily a merchant who commissioned independent craftsmen or skilled laborers to produce his goods. In the knife trade, independent cutlers (called "little mesters" in Sheffield), for example, made knives for their factors that were stamped with his name.

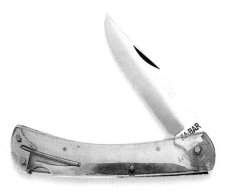

Above *Ka-Bar 1189 folding hunter, cutaway demonstrator model. Note internal music-wire spring.*

OAK LEAF POCKET KNIVES
HOW THEY ARE MADE

POCKET BLADES.

No. 1—Pocket Blade, for No. K2420, Partially Forged; Showing Steel Bar from which it is being Fashioned.

No. 2 — Pocket Blade Forged, Ready for Hardening and Tempering or Grinding.

No. 3—Pocket Blade Ground. Ready for Drilling and Filing, or Drilling and Squaring.

No. 4—Pocket Blade Ready for assembling. Filed and Dressed, or Drilled, Squared and Dressed.

PEN BLADES.

No. 1 — Pen Blade for No. K2420, Partially Forged; Showing Steel Bar from which it is being Fashioned.

No. 2 — Pen Blade Forged, Ready for Hardening and Tempering or Grinding.

No. 3—Pen Blade Ground, Ready for Drilling and Filing, or Drilling and Squaring.

No. 4—Pen Blade Ready for Assembling, Drilled, Filed and Dressed, or Drilled, Squared and Dressed.

No. 5—Spring Steel, from which Spring is Produced.

No. 6—Spring, Dressed and Drilled, Ready for Adjusting.

No. 7—Spring Adjusted, Filed, Hardened, Tempered and Dressed.

No. 8—Sheet Brass, from which Linings are Pressed.

No. 9—German Silver, from which Bolsters are made.

No. 10—Blank for Bolster, Pressed Ready for Stamping.

No. 11—Bolster Stamped up, Ready to Fasten to Lining.

No. 12—Brass Strip, Pierced, Ready to Receive Bolster.

No. 13—Bolsters "Chopped on" Lining, Ready for Passing through Pattern Dies.

No. 14—Scale Pressed, Ready for Drilling.

No. 15—Handle Covering, Ready for Fitting.

No. 16—Covering Fitted, Ready for Name Plate.

No. 17—Name Plates, or Shields, and German Silver from which they are made.

No. 18—Scales, with Covering Fitted, Showing Name Plate and Reverse Side, Ready for Assembling into Handle.

No. 19—Division Scale, or Center Lining.

No. 20—Knife Ready for Final Adjusting—Note Loose Rivets and General Rough Appearance of Knife.

21

Above *One of the many stages in assembling Victorinox "Swiss Army" knives.*

also built in Sheffield between 1823 and 1826; an account of the methods used there, in *The Practical Tourist* by Zachariah Allen, influenced the development of similar factories in the US during the 1830s and 40s, and perhaps explains the peak amount of Sheffield cutlery sold in the US in 1835.

The construction of large cutlery factories naturally led to the rivalry over which was the biggest. Originally, the Sheaf Works factory in Sheffield was the biggest, but it was soon surpassed by the factory built by Joseph Rodgers & Sons in 1850, also in Sheffield. By 1870, the largest cutlery factory in the world was J. Russell & Co.'s in Turner Falls, Massachusetts, which was replaced by Aetna Works (Landers, Frary & Clark) in 1900. This firm took over neighboring Humason & Beckley (H. & B.), which produced the Universal-brand pocketknives until the 1930s. Today, the world's largest cutlery factory is Imperial Schrade's 500,000 square-foot facility in Ellenvile, New York.

Later, as the disadvantages of such "outworking" of labor became clear, many factors converted their warehouses into large workshops where all operations would be carried out simultaneously in the same place, which became the factories as we know them today. The world's first pocketknife manufacturing factories were set up in France during the 18th century. These used water-powered machinery to make mass-produced, inexpensive, folding "penny knives," with no backsprings. Solingen followed, creating the first modern pocket cutlery factory in 1805, but still using the outworking system of independent cutlers for a handcrafted effect, a system still in use to this day. Cutlery factories were

Multiblades and Gadget Knives

For as long as cutlers have been making folding knives, they have been working out ways to include other tools to fit with the blades in the knives' handles. The first step was to include more than one blade, either as insurance against breakage, or to perform a specialized cutting task.

The most obvious non-blade tool that was included in pocketknives was the leather punch, a sharp tool essential for mending broken harnesses.

By the 18th century, cutlers were including an array of specialized blades and tools in folding knives. The ultimate was Joseph Rodgers & Sons "Year Knife," begun in 1822, which had 1,822 different blades, with one more added every year until 1970.

22

• SEQUENCE BOARDS •

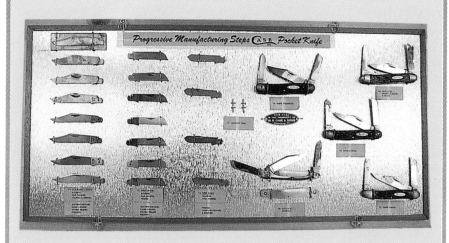

One of the oldest sales aids in cutlers' shops is the "sequence-of-manufacture" board. A sequence board is a series of identical knives, or the component parts thereof, each carried one step nearer to completion than the previous one. The first steps in a sequence board usually show the cutler's raw materials: bars or strips of steel, nickel silver, and brass, often along with assorted handle materials. The last step is usually the finished cutlery item. In between, each piece or assembly fixed to the board demonstrates one or more stages in the manufacturing process.

These boards were used to sell individual knives to consumers, as well as the manufacturer's entire line of knives to retailers. Many manufacturers and distributors displayed sequence boards in their factory showrooms and regional sales offices, and in their showcases of wares on exhibit at expositions, trade shows, and world fairs. Original sequence boards are one of the items most sought after by knife collectors.

This sequence board from W. R. Case & Sons of Bradford, Pennsylvania, is shown here courtesy of its present owner, Smoky Mountain Knife Works in Sevierville, Tennessee, which has hundreds of antique cutlery–advertising items on public display.

• FOLDING KNIVES •

These are some of the blades and tools used in folding knives:

Leather punch • Harness mending bolts • Belt punch • Gimlet • Awl • Typesetter's punch • Quill pen blade • Pen machine • Letter opener • Marlinespike • Rope blade • Weaver's hook • Seam ripper • Button hook • Manicure blade and file • Corn blade • Scissors • Spatula or palette knife • Saw for bone and wood • Metal saw • Cockspur saw • Spey blade • Castrating hook • Seton needle • Scalpel or bistoury • Fleam • Hoof-pick • Dog-stripping comb • Horticultural budding and grafting blade • Grafting spud • Cotton sampling blade • Maize blade • Pruning hook • Pruning shears • Weed digger • Cigar cutter • Cigar punch • Cigar stub fork • Cigar box opener • Cigar box hammer • Pipe tamper • Pipe bowl reamer • Snuff box • Game counter • Dice cup with miniature dice • Silver or gold fruit blade • Silver or gold nut and seed pick • Fork • Spoon • Ear Spoon • Corkscrew • Wire cutter • Whistle •

Pull-out implements in handle

Toothpick • Tweezers • Lancet • Dividers • Cigar punch • Fly-tying vise • Sharpening steel •

Interchangeable Blades for "Tool Kit Knives"

Cutting blades • Files • Saws • Screwdrivers • Gimlet • Punch • Chisel • Ruler • Tin- and bottle-openers • Cork pullers • Hammer •

The following are some of the tools, blades, and gadgets often used in multiblade or gadget-type folding-knife production:

Alligator wrench • Awl • Belt punch • Bird gutting-hook • Bottle-cap lifter • Button cutter • Can opener • Carriage key • Castrating hook • Champagne wire-cutter • Cigar box hammer • Cigar box opener • Cigar cutter • Cigar punch • Cigar stub fork • Cockspur saw • Cork-pulling hook • Corkscrew • Corn blade • Cotton-sampling blade • Crescent wrench • Dagger blade • Dice cup with miniature dice • Dog-stripping comb • Drawing compass • Dynamite-cap crimper • Ear spoon • Electrical-wire stripper • Feeler gauges • Fish gaff • Fish scaler • Fleam • Fly-tying vise • Fork • Fuse cutter • Game counter • Gimlet • Grafting spud • Gutting blade • Harness-mending bolts • Hatchet or cleaver • Hoof pick • Hook disgorger • Hook hone • Horticultural budding and grafting blade • Ink-eraser blade • Key blank • Key-ring • Leather punch • Letter opener • Magnetic compass • Magnifying glass • Maize blade • Manicure blade and file • Marlinespike • Metal saw • Oyster opener • Pencil sharpener • Pen or pencil • Pen machine • Pipe-bowl reamer • Pipe tamper • Pinfire-blank pistol • Pistol • Pliers • "Pres-to-lite" key (for early car headlights) • Pruning hook • Pruning shears • Quill-pen blade • Race • Rope blade • Ruler • Saw for bone and wood • Scalpel or bistoury • Scissors • Screwdriver • Seam ripper • Secton needle • Shotgun-choke tube wrench • Shotgun-shell extractors • Silver- or gold-metal fruit blade • Silver- or gold-metal nut and seed pick • Siren • Skeleton key • Skinning blade • Snuff box • Spatula or palette knife • Spey blade • Spoon • Spring balance • Stanhope lens with miniature photos • Tape measure • Typesetter's punch • Weaver's hook • Weed digger • Whistle • Wire cutter •

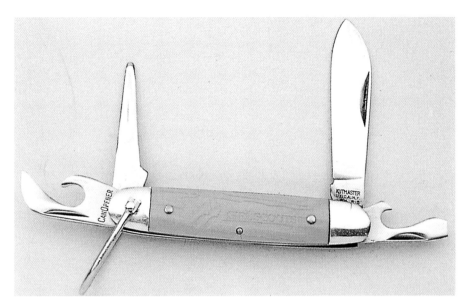

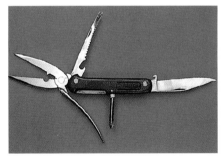

Top *Kutmaster,
3⅜ inches green-
plastic handles with
hot-stamp shield, four
blades.*

Left *German Pirate
logo combination knife,
green horn handles.
Blades: spear master
blade, small
screwdriver/cap-lifter,
lobster manicure blade,
magnifier.*

Above *R. J. Richter,
Germany, angler's
pliers knife, dark red
composition handles
with inset hook hone.
Blades: clip master
blade, fish-scaler/
hook-disgorger/crown
cap-lifter, Phillips
screwdriver, pliers with
split-shot crimper,
tweezers in handle.*

KEYS FOR SUCCESSFUL
POCKETKNIFE COLLECTING

THE SIMPLEST approach to pocketknife collecting can be stated in two sentences: 1) Collect whatever you like; and 2) They're your knives, so do whatever you like with them. However, while you will undoubtedly enjoy this approach, in commercial terms, it will only work if you live on a desert island and will never meet another collector, or if you are so fabulously wealthy that you will never need to sell or trade any of your knives. I know collectors who actually fit both of these descriptions, but as you are not likely to be either, it will behoove you to pay attention to what other collectors may want and expect.

Fashion

Firstly, as we shall see, there are many different types and brands of pocketknives that can be collected, which at any given time may or may not be fashionable among large numbers of enthusiasts and collectors. Fashions are more changeable in modern, handmade knives than they are in antique and classic pocketknives, but the fashions in collecting both do change significantly from time to time.

All it takes to start a fashion is for two aggressive and free-spending collectors to compete for the same type of knives; if their rivalry persists for any length of time, other people will join in, and that particular market niche will take on a life of its own. Sometimes the enthusiasm will survive its original founders; other times, it will not.

Condition

Second in importance for collectors is the condition of the knife. A knife in excellent, *unsharpened* condition is worth much more than one in lesser condition, which knowledgeable collectors will not buy at any price. If you clean or sharpen a knife to "improve" its appearance, you are actually destroying most of its resale value.

Many collectors will only consider knives in "mint" condition. This means knives that have never been used, carried, cleaned, or sharpened. Modern knives, including the handmade, limited-edition, and standard factory ones, are only collectible if they are in mint condition. They may still have value for use as a knife, but that is all. Mint-condition, antique pocketknives are a delicate subject, as are their materials—their blades and springs can rust, their fittings become discolored, or their handle materials shrink or crack—so some collectors shy away from them, since one day of extreme humidity could wipe out their investment. Despite the risks, though, there remains a strong market for antique knives in true mint condition.

Cleaning

The rules of cleaning are simple: 1) When in doubt, don't; and 2) When not in doubt, DEFINITELY don't!

Over-enthusiastic cleaning will destroy whatever remains of a knife's original finish, substantially reducing its value. Also, a

Top row *(Left to right):* recent Schrade barlow knife, smooth-bone handles; Parker Cutlery Co's miniature jackknife, abalone-shell handles; 1980s Case light trapper, red jigged-bone handles.

Middle *Late 19th-century, large Sheffield horseman's multi-blade with stag handles, made for A. G. Alford Sporting Goods Co., Baltimore, MD.*

Bottom row *(Left to right):* Ka-Bar jackknife with razor and spey blades, wood handles; Case serpentine jack, genuine stag handles; Parker Cutlery Co. small lockback with pearl handles.

Right *NKCA (National Knife Collectors Association) 1992 Club Knife, trapper pattern made by Queen Cutlery Co.*

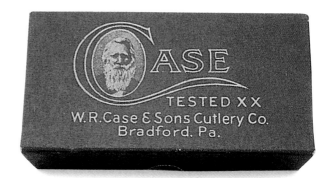

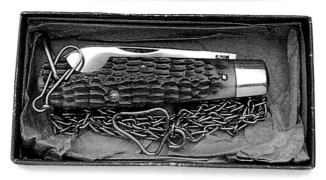

Right *Case "Tested XX" easy-open, barehead, standard jack with shackle and chain, jigged-bone handles, and original box.*

cautious buyer will assume that a heavily cleaned knife has been reworked, even if it has not. Cautious buyers only buy originals —never knives they suspect are reworks. Apply this principle to your own purchasing.

There are a few exceptions, however—for example, fingerprints should be gently wiped off with a soft, clean cloth. A drop of light machine oil or Japanese sword oil can be applied to the joint of each blade, but never use lubricants containing solvents or dryers, such as 3-in-1 Oil or WD-40. Clean lint and grease from handles, using a wooden toothpick, and use oil and a sharp needle to remove spots of active (red) rust. However, if you care about the historical, esthetic, or monetary value of a knife, don't do anything else to it.

Storage

This is a difficult topic, even for museums. The most important factors are stable temperature and humidity; acid-free containers and atmosphere; and protection from Dermestid carpet beetles, which devour horn and other organic materials. You can get acid-free paper and cardboard from picture framers, and acid-free boxes from museum supply firms. The rooms where knives are stored must be climate-controlled for both temperature and humidity; bank vaults are usually safe if the bank is air-conditioned.

Some collectors store knives in open boxes or wrapped up protective, "tarnish-proof" cloth; both methods can either work

Right *Reading is a good way to further your knowledge of pocketknives. Pictured here are* Levine's Guide, *1985 edition (the 3rd edition was published in 1993), and J. Bruce Voyle's* Antique Knives *(see Further Reading).*

or fail miserably. Museums generally use open boxes, since sometimes knives stored in closed boxes can rust away to nothing. However, never store knives inside leather sheaths or purses, as these can deteriorate and affect the condition of the knife. Some deluxe-edition, antique knives came with elegant, clasp-top or snap-flap knife purses, which should be preserved without the knives inside them. Make sure that wherever you store your knives, you check them regularly for any sign of deterioration.

Learning

The best thing you can do to learn about knives is what you are doing now—reading about them. If you wish to read more, see the "Further Reading" section on page 74.

Another valuable way to learn about knives is to go to knife shows, knife shops, and museums with good knife collections in their exhibitions, such as the National Knife Museum in Chattanooga, Tennessee; the American Military Edged Weaponry Museum in Intercourse, Pennsylvania; the Sheffield City Museum, in Sheffield, England; and the Solingen Blade Museum in Solingen, Germany. The Smithsonian Museum of American History in Washington, DC and the Victoria & Albert Museum in London, England have important knife collections, but as these are not usually on display, special arrangements must be made to view them.

At knife shows and in shops, remember not to open more than one blade at a time when handling an antique folding knife.

POCKETKNIFE IDENTIFIER

THE MOST POPULAR POCKETKNIFE BRANDS

A POCKETKNIFE'S STORY can be read on its blade's tangs—the unsharpened extension fixed into the knife's handle. Blade tangs are usually stamped with the name or trademark of the firm that distributed the knife, whether the manufacturer, or its importer, wholesaler, or retailer. This is important, because although a knife may have value in itself, most collectors care passionately about the brand names stamped on its tangs, since some brands made better quality knives. Brands also matter to those who like to collect things in complete sets, as a knife's brand can tell them if it "belongs" with their other knives. Also, the knife's brand indicates its approximate age, and where and how it was sold—through mail order, jewelry shops, hardware shops, cutlery shops, department stores, sports shops, traveling salesmen, or as a promotional item—and even who bought it originally.

Above *Large Case store display knife, 11¼ inches long closed, slick, black, composition handles.*

Top *Case XX USA 6-dot (1974) premium jack, red jigged-bone handles.*

• W. R. CASE & SONS BLADE-TANG STAMPINGS •

The Case brand has been phenomenally popular in the US for over 25 years, probably because in the 1960s, when collecting pocketknives first became popular, Case still offered a diverse, high-quality line of traditional designs with deluxe, natural handles such as pearl and stag. Because Case changed its blade-tang stampings regularly over the years, it is easy for collectors to date them. Also, the knives were widely available, although of the over-75 tang stampings from the original Case firms, a few are very rare, and only interest advanced collectors.

Case/Bradford, PA This was used as a 2-line tang stamping from 1905–1920. Some recent reissue "collector" knives also bear this stamping, but their materials and finish identify them as modern.

Case/Tested XX The "C" in the brand name is larger than the other letters, and often continued to form an underline beneath the "ASE." Called "Circle C" or "Tested" by collectors, this mark (or slight variations of it), was standard from around 1920–1940 or 41. This brand is widely counterfeited, so beware (see "Counterfeits" section, p. 69).

Case/XX Called "Double X" by collectors, this two-line mark was standard on Case pocketknives from the postwar resumption of commercial marketing in 1945 through 1965.

Case XX/row of dots with runic "SS" in center/
USA Called "Lightning S" by collectors, the runic "SS" stands for "stainless steel," and the amount of dots specify the year the knife was made, starting from 1890 through to 1990 (10 dots = 1980; 9 dots = 1981; etc.).

*Other versions (not pictured) include **Case XX/Made in USA** (1965–1970; called "Case USA" by collectors) and **Case XX/Made in USA/above a tiny row of dots** (1970–1980), with the dots indicating the year of manufacture (10 dots = 1970; 9 dots = 1980, etc.). These are referred to as "ten dot," "nine dot," etc. by collectors.

1905–1920   **1920–1940/41**   **1945–1965**   **1980–1990**

The following section introduces you to some of the most popular brands of knives, and also various styles of knives produced. These include some of the most famous brands in the US and Europe, as well as some of the more specialty-type knives.

Famous American Brands

• Case Brothers/W. R. Case & Sons

The original Case Bros. firm was formed in 1896 when three Case brothers—Jean, John, and Andrew—began a wholesale cutlery

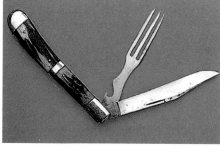

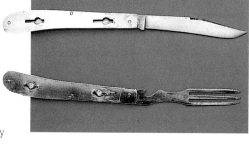

Above *Western States Cutlery Co., Boulder, CO, "Dox Fish Gaff" angler's knife.*

Right *Union Cutlery Co., Olean, NY, Model 2291 K&F "slot knife" take-apart knife and fork, with genuine stag handles.*

firm in Little Valley, New York. Although their designs were at first contracted out, by 1900 they were manufacturing their own knives, straight razors, and hones. This lasted until 1915, but in 1902, their nephew, J. Russell Case, opened his own firm in Little Valley, naming it W. R. Case & Sons Cutlery Co. He later opened a different factory with H. N. Platts in Bradford, Pennsylvania, and the knives made there excite the greatest interest today.

• Western States Cutlery Co.

This firm originated in New York in 1896, when an emigrant cutler from Sheffield, Charles W. Platts, who had been working for the Northfield Knife Co., decided to start his own pocketknife company. "C. W. Platts & Sons" was taken over in 1900 by his second son, Harvey Nixon Platts, who moved the company to Boulder, Colorado, and changed its name to "Western States Cutlery and Manufacturing Co." In 1920, the company began the first pocketknife

manufacturing in the American West, adding hunting knives to its product range in 1928. It changed names again between 1956 and 1990, first to "Western Cutlery Co." and then to "Coleman-Western," but its most popular products predate 1941.

• Union Cutlery Co.

Wallace and Emerson Brown began manufacturing and importing pocketknives and razors under the name Brown Bros. Mfg. Co. in Tidioute, Pennsylvania in 1890, later changing the company's name to Union Cutlery Co. The firm moved to a new factory in Olean, New York, in 1912, where it enjoyed great success through its association with the Case Bros. firm with pocketknives and hunting knives produced under the trademark "KA-BAR" (see following entry).

• KA-BAR/Kabar Cutlery Co.

The name "KA-BAR" is commonly associated with the US Marine Corps 1219C2 (Navy Mark 2) combat knife, introduced in 1943, which was developed by Camillus but bore the KA-BAR stamping; both Camillus and KA-BAR versions of this design are still sold commercially.

There are also some classic, larger KA-BAR knives whose front handles are inlaid with a shield in the shape of a dog's head. Union Cutlery's trademark KA-BAR name was changed to Kabar Cutlery Co. in 1951, which is a watershed date for collectors, since later stampings are considered less desirable. The older "KA-BAR" stamping is still used on limited reissues of classic knives, but the current Kabar-brand knives are either made under contract, or are imported. Kabar Cutlery became a division of Cole National Corp. in Cleveland, Ohio in 1966; its other brands include Khyber, Sabre, and Monarch.

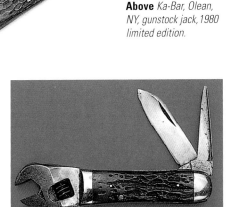

Above *Ka-Bar, Olean, NY, gunstock jack, 1980 limited edition.*

• Cattaraugus Cutlery Co.

This Little Valley, New York-based firm began as J.B.F. Champlin & Son, a wholesale importer of German cutlery. In 1886, the founder changed the name to Cattaraugus (after the county's name), and began manufacturing cutlery as a supplement to their imports. This included pocketknives, razors, scissors, and, in 1925, hunting knives. The latter were produced as a joint venture between Case and Cattaraugus in the Kinfolks factory in Little Valley, which later became an independent company also producing pocketknives. Cattaraugus was famous for its WWII 225Q "Commando" knives, aircrew-survival folding machetes, and TL-29 electrician's knives, with their innovative "liner-lock." Cattaraugus also made the knives for Admiral Richard E. Byrd's Antarctic expeditions. Later, the

Above *Cattaraugus Cutlery Co., Little Valley, NY, crescent wrench-knife stag-bone handles.*

company mainly made fixed-blade kitchen knives with black, plastic handles and chrome-plated blades; its products are now less popular among collectors than 10–15 years ago.

• Robeson Cutlery Co.

Millard Robeson first sold imported knives from his home in Elmira, New York, but in 1894, began to manufacture his own knives, eventually building factories in Rochester

Right *Pal Blade Co.,
Plattsburgh, NY, easy-
open, swell-end jack,
bronze handles, with
leftover Remington
pen blade (made
c1940–1942).*

Below *Robeson No-
Rustain lockback
English jack with
folding guard.*

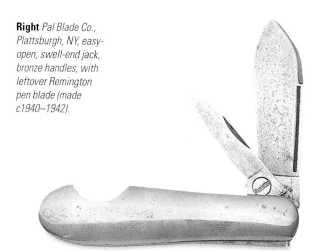

Remington U.M.C./Pal Blade Co.

Beginning in 1920, the Remington Arms–Union Metallic Cartridge Company produced pocketknives along with WWI ammunition in an ultra-modern factory in Bridgeport, Connecticut, but by 1925, its cutlery division had become the dominant maker of top-quality pocketknives in the USA. At its peak in 1931, the company was producing over 10,000 high-quality pocketknives a day, with over 1,000 different patterns (also hunting knives, household cutlery, and advertising and promotional materials that are as avidly collected as the knives themselves). In 1940, the company stopped cutlery production to resume work on defense materials, and its cutlery division was sold to Pal Blade Co. in Plattsburgh, New York. However, because of its previous glory and the famous name's link to gun collecting, Remington is one of the most sought-after brands today.

and Perry and New York to produce his "Shuredge"-brand pocketknives. When Emerson Case (grandson of W.R.) became president of the company in 1940, he increased its prosperity by introducing stainless-steel blades, now used in all pocketknife production. Robeson stopped manufacturing in 1960, but continued to sell contract-made Robeson knives until 1977. Robeson knives are not as valuable as Case of KA-BAR.

• REMINGTON BULLETS •

• R1123: 4½-inch-large trapper, bone handle • R1128: 4½-inch trapper, wood handle • R1173: "Baby Bullet," 3½-inch-large trapper, bone handle • R1253: 5½-inch, curved, regular, lockback hunting knife, bone handle • R1263: 5⅜-inch, curved, regular jack, clip-master blade, bone handle • R1273: 5⅜-inch, curved, regular jack, spear-master blade, bone handle • R1306: 4⅝-inch, swell-center hunting knife, stag handle • R1303: 4½-inch, swell-center hunting knife, bone handle • R1613: 5-inch tickler, bone handle • R4243: 4¾-inch-large, four-blade utility knife, bone handle • R4353: 4½-inch, double-end trapper, bone handle • R4466: 3⅝-inch, double-end trapper, stag handle •

• Remington Bullets

In 1922, Remington introduced the first of two dozen patterns of large, stout, sportsman's folding knives, each with a shield in the shape of a high-power rifle cartridge—hence the collector's name of "Remington Bullets." The initial "bullet" knife, the R1123 large trapper with jigged-bone handles, is the most popular, with the wood-handled version (the R1128), based on a German design made by the Solingen-born cutler who worked for Remington in 1919 being a close second. The other ten "bullet" designs (see box) are much rarer; there are also variants using blade etch, bone jigging, etc., which are sought by advanced collectors. In 1982, replicas of the R1123 with plastic handles proved very successful, and Remington have since issued a new replica "bullet knife" every year. These are now nearly as rare and valuable as the originals.

Above *Remington 1993 "Bullet" knife.*

Right *Remington "Bullet" R4466 double-end trapper, genuine stag handles.*

• REVOLUTION GOES UNDERGROUND •

Remington and Winchester both experimented with modernizing the manufacturing process after World War I. Remington tried to eliminate the extra steps and uncertain results of "chopping on" bolsters to handles by substituting integral, drop-forged handle frames, while Winchester attempted to substitute forging in their first blades with blanked-and-ground, chrome-vanadium tool steel for forged, high-carbon steel. But neither firms' techniques were accepted by professional hardware buyers, who refused to tolerate new pocketknife technology, thus forcing both firms to revert to their original procedures. However, both firms did continue to develop new technology, but this time they ensured that it did not show. Today, most pocketknife firms continue to hide most of their technological innovations under a veneer of traditional appearance.

Original Winchester pocketknives are nearly the quality of Remingtons, except for the cheap "assortment knives" made during the Depression. However, they are as popular among collectors as Remingtons, and are equally valuable.

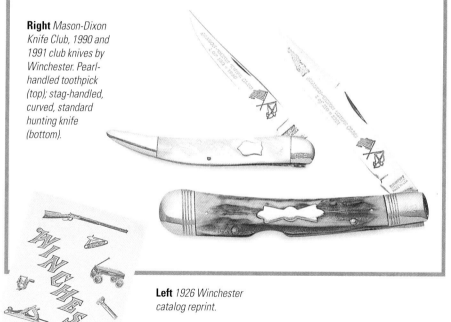

Right *Mason-Dixon Knife Club, 1990 and 1991 club knives by Winchester. Pearl-handled toothpick (top); stag-handled, curved, standard hunting knife (bottom).*

Left *1926 Winchester catalog reprint.*

• Winchester

Originally a firearms company based in New Haven, Connecticut, Winchester went into the cutlery business after World War I, buying out existing cutlery firms and employing skilled staff from the Napanoch Knife Co., New York (a major, private-brand contractor founded in 1901), which provided a range of premium patterns. The Eagle Knife Co. in New Haven, which provided the technology for mass production had been founded in 1916 by the Heming Brothers, who had invented the first successful automatic grinder in 1903, many of which are still in use.

• E. C. Simmons—"Keen Kutter" and "Oak Leaf"

The best-known and most successful US wholesale hardware firm was the E. C. Simmons Hardware Co. of St. Louis, Missouri, established in 1868. It was the first company to become incorporated, allowing employee profit sharing, and also the first to produce an illustrated catalog

• Reissue Winchesters •

In 1985, Winchester authorized Blue Grass Cutlery Co. of Manchester, Ohio to sell new knives with the Winchester trademark. These are produced by Queen Cutlery Co., Utica, and Camillus in traditional patterns, with natural-material handles. These reissue knives are attractive and well made, and have a devoted following among collectors. Both Winchester-Germany and Winchester-France (national distribution agencies for the firms firearms), offer modern-style knives with the Winchester logo; these are made in Germany, Italy, and Japan, and although not sold in the US, are available in Europe.

Above *Two E. C. Simmons "Keen Kutter" pearl-handled penknives: a four-blade shadow congress (top), and a senator with tip bolsters (bottom).*

Left *Winchester 2877 muskrat.*

Below *New York Knife Co., Walden, NY, Model 135 rase knife with cocobolo handles.*

Left *Queen Cutlery Co., Titusville, PA, sleeveboard jack, Winterbottom-bone handles.*

Below *Ulster Knife Co., Ellenville, NY, senator pen, tip bolsters, bail to hang knife from watch chain, jigged-bone handles.*

(1881). Simmons bought key manufacturers to control the costs and supply of his two most popular brands of pocketknives, the "Keen Kutter" and "Oak Leaf" brands, making a huge profit by selling private-brand merchandise to other firms. Simmons also acquired the Walden Knife Co. (Walden, New York) in 1902, and additional Simmons brands, including the "Hornet" and "William Enders Oak Leaf," were obtained from Germany. Simmons merged with Winchester in 1922, but was later absorbed by its long-term rival, Shapleigh Hardware Co.

• New York Knife Co.—"Hammer" and "Walkill River Works" Prior to Remington, New York Knife Co. in Walden, New York (originally founded in 1852 by Sheffield *emigrés*) was the leading supplier of high-quality pocketknives to wholesale markets, both under its popular "Hammer" brand and other house-brand names. The company was the first to make the official Boy Scout knives, and also produced cheap, mass-produced, English-style knives with the

"Walkill River Works" logo. The firm went out of business in 1930, and its "Hammer" logo was taken over by Imperial.

• Queen Cutlery Co./Schatt & Morgan
The company's original founders, J. W. Schatt and C. B. Morgan, began as cutlery importers and jobbers in New York, where they opened a factory under their joint names. They later relocated to Titusville, Pennsylvania (known as the "Queen City"), where some of their supervisors set up the Queen City Cutlery Co. on the side, using Schatt & Morgan's components. By the time they were caught and fired, S & M was bankrupt, and Queen City took over its assets, changing its company name to Queen Cutlery Co. While Queen and Original S & M knives are popular with

collectors, Queen is best known today as the contract manufacturer of some KA-BAR, reissue Winchesters, and the Case Heritage series, also producing reissue S & M knives for collectors.

• Ulster Knife Co.

In 1871, a group of Sheffield cutlers formed the Cooperative Knife Co. in Ulster County, New York. When this company failed, it was reorganized in 1876 under local banker Dwight Divine as the Ulster Knife Co., and soon became a leading, private-brand contractor of high-quality knives. It continued to use Sheffield-style handcrafted methods and quality up to 1941 despite the loss of profits, but was inevitably forced to sell. Albert M. Baer bought the company and brought in specialists, who succeeded in transforming Ulster into the most modern cutlery plant in the world.

• Kingston Cutlery Co.

After Pearl Harbor, all US cutlery firms were coordinated to make millions of knives for the armed forces by the Army Advisory Board. In 1943, Albert Baer of Ulster Knife Co. and the owners of Imperial Knife Co. formed a joint venture called Kingston Knife Co., after an Ulster brand. Kingston produced utility knives throughout the war, later taking over Schrade Cutlery Co.

Above *Kingston (joint venture of Ulster and Imperial) utility knife made for the US Marine Corps, World War II.*

Top *Kingston (joint venture of Ulster and Imperial) utility knife made for the US Army, World War II.*

• Schrade Cutlery Co.

George Schrade, founder of the Schrade Cutlery Co. in Walden, New York, was one of the most prolific inventors in American cutlery history. His "Press-Button" knife, introduced in 1892, was the first switchblade suited to mass-production methods; he also invented and

Left *Schrade Cutlery Co., Walden, NY, Safety "Push-Button" Knife, with celluloid handles.*

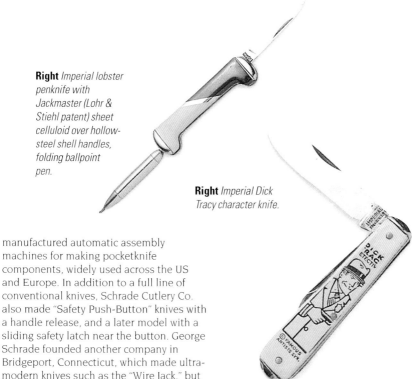

Right *Imperial lobster penknife with Jackmaster (Lohr & Stiehl patent) sheet celluloid over hollow-steel shell handles, folding ballpoint pen.*

Right *Imperial Dick Tracy character knife.*

manufactured automatic assembly machines for making pocketknife components, widely used across the US and Europe. In addition to a full line of conventional knives, Schrade Cutlery Co. also made "Safety Push-Button" knives with a handle release, and a later model with a sliding safety latch near the button. George Schrade founded another company in Bridgeport, Connecticut, which made ultra-modern knives such as the "Wire Jack," but these are less interesting to collectors than those of the original Schrade company.

• Imperial Knife Co.
This company was formed 1916 in Providence, Rhode Island by two Italian immigrants who had worked for Empire Knife Co. in Connecticut. During WWI, they made vast numbers of little "IKCO"-brand jackknives for the US Navy, but later specialized in "skeleton knives" fitted with gold or silver handles by jewelers, and low-cost, mass-produced jackknives with fancy handles, popular today with cost-conscious collectors. In the late 1930s, Imperial licensed the technology for making cheap pocketknives with hollow sheet-steel

handles and covered with sheet celluloid from Solingen inventor Ernst Lohr, steadily improving this technology in the next two decades. By the 1940s, Imperial was producing 100,000 "Jackmaster, Hammer Brand" knives a day, replaced by "Diamond Edge" knives in the 1960s. Their merger with Ulster Knife Co. and Shrade in 1943 under the title "Imperial Knife Associated Companies" made them the world's current leading cutlery manufacturer.

• Camillus Cutlery Co.
In 1902, Adolph Kastor, a leading New York City cutlery importer and wholesaler, bought

Right *Two A. W. Wadsworth & Sons (Austrian-made) deerfoot folding knives, imported by Adolph Kastor & Bros., New York, from Bohemia prior to World War I.*

Below *Camillus recent, small, rope knife.*

Above *Camillus waiter's knife, all metal.*

a small pocketknife plant in Camillus, New York. Through diligent salesmanship of private-brand knives to emerging mass-market retail chains—Sears Roebuck & Co. (Sta-Sharp, Kwik-Kut, and Dunlap brands), F. W. Woolworth (Kent brand), and K-Mart (originally Kresge)—Camillus soon became the leading US contract maker of private brands, a position it still holds. Camillus

was also the leading maker of US character and figural pocketknives (see pp. 55–58) in the 1930s and 40s, and has been a leading supplier of deluxe advertising knives for companies such as Anheuser Busch and Coca-Cola; today, it makes the most-popular limited-edition knives, including reissue Remingtons and wildlife or other collector specials.

• **Utica Cutler Co.—"Kutmaster" and "Jack Knife Ben"** Though not as large or well known as some of its rivals, the Utica Cutlery Co. from upstate New York has been an important pocket cutlery firm since 1910. Its many well-known trademark brands include "Agate Wood," "American Maid," "Featherweight," "Iroquois," "Seneca," and "Pocket Pard," but the best-known brand by far was the "Kutmaster," adopted in 1937. The company has long been an active private-brand contractor with Chicago-based retailers, and is known for its production of "Wards" brand pocketknives for Montgomery Wards, and its famous "Jack Knife Ben" knives, which are in great demand by collectors. Today, the company specializes in pocketknives with coined-metal handles, both under its own name and under contract.

• **Gerber Legendary Blades**
In 1939, Joseph R. Gerber, an advertising man in Portland, Oregon, designed his first carving knife, which led him to open a factory producing carving and steak knives with cast-aluminum handles. Since the 1960s, Gerber began to make hunting knives, combat-survival knives, and "Fh" model folding hunters, in three-handle and two-blade metal variations; the tool-steeled, checkered-walnut-handle version is very popular with Japanese collectors. The "Fh" was later replaced with the metal-framed Folding Sportsman series, including presentation-boxed knives with semiprecious-stone inlays. Gerber also imports smaller, folding knives from Japan, marketed under the name "Silver Knight," and "Gerber-Paul" button-lock, folding knives, much in demand among US collectors. The company is now owned by Fiskars cutlery firm in Helsinki, Finland.

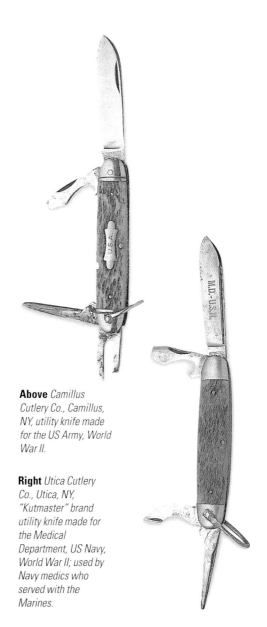

Above *Camillus Cutlery Co., Camillus, NY, utility knife made for the US Army, World War II.*

Right *Utica Cutlery Co., Utica, NY, "Kutmaster" brand utility knife made for the Medical Department, US Navy, World War II; used by Navy medics who served with the Marines.*

43

Below *Presentation-boxed, Gerber folding sportsman with engraved-brass frame and green jade-handle inlays.*

Other Leading US Brands

The following knives and firms, while not as large as the others detailed in this section, are nevertheless very important to knife collectors for some of their distinguished contributions to the pocketknife industry.

• J. Russell & Co.—"Russell barlows"
One of the first-recorded cutlery factories in the US, the Greenfield River Works in Greenfield, Massachusetts, was built in 1834 by John Russell—maker of the famous J. Russell & Co. barlow knives. These were so popular, especially in the South, that nearly every hardware and cutlery firm offered a selection. The firm made various knives until it merged with Harrington Cutlery in 1933; its last, authentic "Russell barlow" was made in 1941. The knife's popularity lives on—for example, to be a member of the "Barlow Bearcats" in Louisville, Kentucky, the only requirement is the ownership of a genuine Russell barlow knife.

• "Buck knives"
Another popular US knife is the "Buck Knife," a generic term deriving from the original Buck's Model 110 folding hunting knife with handmade, fixed blades, produced in the Washington-state factory of

Alfred and Charles Buck in 1962. Their ancestor, Hoyt Heath Buck, had made the first Buck knives with fixed blades early in the century, and while they created their model as an improvement to his design, they were surprised at the knife's success and wide-ranging appeal. However, the Model 110, with its sturdy, lock-back, folding mechanism, has now sold millions, and is the most successful new knife design of all time, as well as the most copied.

• Al Mar Knives and Kershaw Cutlery Co.
These two companies were both founded by former Gerber employees in the 1970s, and primarily import knives from Japan, sold under the name Silver Knight. Their knives are sold around the world, and attract a lot of interest from collectors.

Hardware Wholesalers

Hardware wholesaler "house brands" are an up-and-coming specialty in pocketknife collecting, largely because of their historical value. The evolution of hardware distribution was a key chapter in the economic development of North America, with its heyday lasting from 1840–1940, a time when every American and Canadian city from the established East-coast states

Below *Belknap Hardware "John Primble"- brand muskrat.*

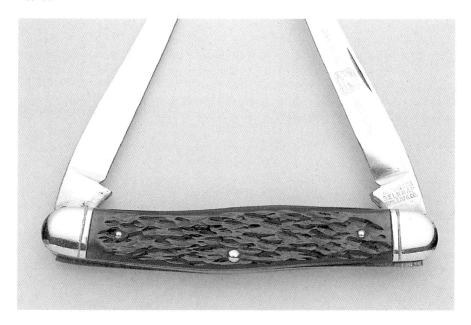

to the developing, Western-frontier states had at least two or three wholesale hardware firms. These supplied local hardware and general merchandise shops within a 100-mile radius with a wide array of goods, usually on very generous credit terms. This often allowed local merchants the means to supply rural customers with the latest products available in more urban locations.

Some of these larger firms later became giant hardware wholesale firms, with nationwide and international distribution. The bigger firms had access to all the major technological revolutions, such as the inventions of the steamboat, railway, telegraph, and telephone, which allowed

salesmen to travel and communicate widely in pursuit of promoting and selling their goods. The access to mass production, which had begun in 1798, boomed after 1865, increasing the amount of goods for sale, and printed, illustrated catalogs increased their distribution further.

• Private Brands
By the 1870s, wholesale territories increasingly overlapped, intensifying the competition. Hardware distributors began putting their own brand names on merchandise they sold, especially cutlery, which was a very profitable, high-value line. This helped to develop brand loyalty with both consumers and retailers.

Right *Shapleigh Hardware Co.'s "Diamond-Edge" -brand muskrat.*

Below *Reprint of a 1925 KA-BAR catalogue sheet. The "Grizzly" is a large, stag-handled, clasp type switchblade.*

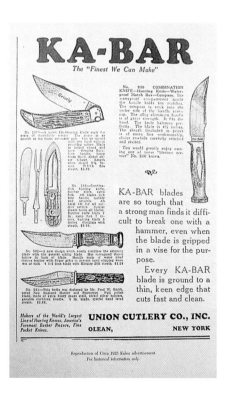

• HARDWARE BRANDS •

• "Keen Kutter," "William Enders Oak Leaf," "Chipaway," "Hornet" (*E. C. Simmons Hardware Co.*, St. Louis, MO; branches at Philadelphia, PA, Toledo, OH, Sioux City, IA, Minneapolis, MN, and Wichita, KS) • "Diamond Edge," "Bridge" (*Shapleigh Hardware Co.*, St. Louis, MO owned "Keen Kutter" brand after 1940) • John Primble India Steel Works," "Blue Grass," "Pine Knot" (*Belknap Hardware Co.*, Louisville, KY) • "Our Very Best," "True Value" (*Hibbard, Spencer Bartlett & Co.*, Chicago, IL—now True Value Hardware Stores) • "Zenith," "Hartford" (*Marshall Wells Hardware Co.*, Duluth, MN; branches at Portland, OR, Spokane, WA, Billings, MT, Great Falls, MT, USA, and at Winnipeg, MB, Edmonton, AB, and Vancouver, BC, Canada) • "Henry Sears 1865" (*Farwell Ozmun Kirk & Co.*, St. Paul, MN) • "Stiletto," Damascus," "Golden Gate" (*Baker Hamilton & Pacific*, San Francisco, CA; sales offices around the Pacific Rim) • "Clean Cut," "Springbrooke" (*Dunham, Carrigan & Hayden*, San Francisco, CA) • "Red Devil" (*Smith & Hemenway*, Utica, NY) •

• CUTLERY WHOLESALERS •

Specialized wholesale cutlery firms played almost as large a role in 19th-century American cutlery distribution as the wholesale hardware companies did. Before the Civil War, there were dozens of firms, whose salesmen sold English, German, and American cutlery to retailers and wholesalers across the US. By the 1890s, a few firms (mostly based in New York City) had become dominant, the most notable of which were: George Borgfeldt; Butler Bros.; F. A. Clauberg & Co.; Coast Cutlery; J. Curley & Bros.; Graef & Schmidt; J. S. Holler; R. J. Roberts; Vom Cleff & Co.; and Wester Bros. Since World War II, specialized cutlery wholesaling has continued to prosper. Some wholesale firms promote their own private brands, but most distribute a variety of widely advertised manufacturers' brands. The most important cutlery wholesaler firms are the following:

Boker

The oldest American wholesale cutlery firm still in business today is Heinrich Boker & Co., established in 1837 by German immigrants in New York. It has branches in Canada, Germany, and Mexico, and has its own factories in Solingen and New Jersey. The German branch is now the parent company.

Kastor

The largest US wholesaler was Adolph Kastor & Bros., founded in 1876. Its Germania Cutlery Works in Solingen operated as a factor commissioning American-style cutlery to be made by Solingen craftsmen and factories. In 1902, Kastor bought and expanded the Camillus Cutlery Co. as a source of tariff-free, American-made knives; in addition to the many brands produced under Camillus' name, Kastor trademarks included "Clover," "Imperial Razor Co.," "Cutwell," "Germania," "A. W. Wadsworth," "W. H. Morley," "J. Koester's Sons," "Duane Cutlery Co.," "Ebro," "XLNT," "Pathfinder," and "Big Chief." The Kastor name and most of these brands were last used in 1947.

Wiebusch & Hilger

In 1864, William Hilger and Frederick Wiebusch, originally from the wholesale hardware business, bought factories in Sheffield, Germany, and Nixdorf, Bohemia (a major pocketknife center before WWI), later building the Challenge Cutlery Co. in Bridgeport, Connecticut. Their brands included "Atlantic," "Western," "Monumental," "Walter Bros.," "Princeton," "Owl," and "Challenge." Charles Wiesbusch's extensive and unmatched knife collection is now in the Smithsonian Institution.

Below *Boker 2¾ inches, all-metal handles, etched Girl Scout emblem on handle, one blade.*

Below *Remington UMC dog-stripping knife, stag-bone handles.*

By World War I, there were dozens of private hardware, house-cutlery brands across the US and Canada. Most were local or regional, but some were better known nationally than most manufacturers' brands, and these (especially the "Keen Kutter" trademark) are highly collectible today. Some collectors specialize in obscure brands, or those from their own city or region. This private-brand pocket cutlery for the hardware houses was usually made by contract manufacturers in the US and Germany, since the US Tariff Act of 1891 barred Sheffield cutlery firms from producing for the American market. This was one of the reasons that thousands of Sheffield and Solingen cutlers emigrated to the US; they comprised a large percentage of the staff of many of the private-brand contractors, particularly the New York Knife Co. and Ulster Knife Co.

Since 1922, the dominant American pocketknife contractor has been Camillus, followed by Utica, Queen, and Alcas (maker of "Cutco" household knives).

• Remington and the Demise of the US Wholesale Hardware Business When

Remington Arms entered the pocketknife business, it did no private-brand work, but pioneered worldwide marketing of their own "Remington UMC" brand, now one of the most collectible. Hardware houses in every state and nation jumped on this bandwagon, abandoning their house brands in favor of the presold Remington line.

The Depression weeded out the weaker, less flexible hardware houses, the ones that were undercapitalized or that failed to adapt to changing times. It also bankrupted Remington, which had extended credit to all of the houses, but the company was saved when it was taken over by DuPont in 1933.

What really killed the wholesale hardware business was World War II—four long years of virtually zero business. And Remington, which had been the mainstay knife line, abruptly dropped out of the cutlery business in 1940, leaving a vacuum that no other knife firm was able to fill. Even the strong hardware firms that did survive the war found the whole world changed after 1945—diversity and high quality had nearly vanished from cutlery manufacture; markets were flooded with military-surplus knives; once-famous brand names had been forgotten by the fickle public; and the population in general was concentrating in the bigger cities and their suburbs. A few hardware houses adapted by developing suburban markets, following the "Winchester Store" model that had been pioneered—prematurely, as it turned out— by Winchester-Simmons in the 1920s. Today,

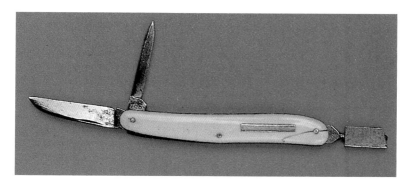

Above *Ivory-handled shadow-wharncliffe knife by John Nowill & Sons of Sheffield, incorporating a folding diamond-glass cutter by Sharrat & Newth.*

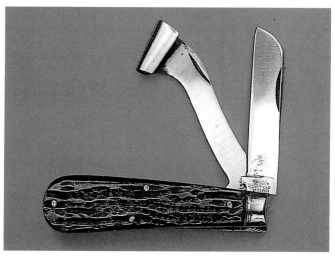

Right *Wade & Butcher, Sheffield, England, race knife (timber scriber) with auxiliary sheepfoot blade, stag-bone handles.*

"True Value" is the best-known retailer network, but it does not sell private-brand knives. However, most of the great, old hardware wholesalers just faded away.

English Brands

Although the pocket-cutlery industry was developed in England long before the American Revolution, from that time until 1891, its fortunes were inextricably intertwined with that of the United States—nowhere more so than in Sheffield, the English center of the trade. Despite the Revolution, Sheffield remained the source for the US of most of its high-quality cutlery, blade, spring, and tool steel, steel-making technology and capital, and thousands of skilled workmen (many of whom had emigrated to the US, bringing their Old-World skills with them). In return, America was Sheffield's largest export market.

The steep tariffs introduced by the US in 1891, and increased in 1901 and steadily after, put an end to this mutually beneficial trading relationship, as many of Sheffield's

Major Sheffield
• Cutlery Firms •

A list of Sheffield cutlers and cutlery firms whose knives were sold in the United States would fill an entire book, but these are some of the most prominent (courtesy Geoffrey Tweedale): Joseph Rodgers & Sons • George Wostenholm & Son • Naylor & Sanderson • John Sorby & Sons • Marsh Brothers • William Greaves & Sons • Benjamin James Eyre & Co. • Frederick Ward & Co. • William & Samuel Butcher (Wade & Butcher) • Thomas Turner & Company • (Wade) Wingfield Rowbotham & Co. • Joseph Haywood • William Gilchrist • Wilson, Hawksworth & Moss (& Ellison) • Mappin Brothers • Henry Barge • John Hinchcliffe • Unwin & Rodgers • Richard Bunting • Jonathan Crookes & Son • Sleigh Rowland • Luke Booth • Henry C. Booth • Samuel Wragg & Sons • George Woodhead • John Askham • Broomhead & Thomas • James Westa • John Coe • Brookes & Crookes • Harrison Brothers & Howson • Herbert M. Slater • Charles Ibbotson • George Hides & Son • Champion & Co. • Michael Hunter & Son • George Ibberson & Co. •

premier pocket-cutlery firms were hurt by this additional burden. Nevertheless, the US pocket cutlery trade was indelibly affected by its links with Sheffield, and this has helped to increase the city's fame in the posterity of pocketknife production.

• George Wostenholm & Son—"I*XL"

This cutlery company was originally founded near Sheffield by George Wostenholme in 1745. His business was passed on to his grandson, George, who shortened the family name to "Wostenholm," and continued producing cutlery in the Rockingham Works workshop in Sheffield. It was his son (also called "George") who registered the famous "I*XL" ("I excel") trademark in 1826, and in 1830, sent a consignment of his cutlery with a leading factor and exporter, Naylor & Sanderson, to investigate the growing US markets. This venture proved so successful that the Wostenholms decided to concentrate all their efforts on creating cutlery for the US, and subsequently moved the firm into a very large and modern factory called the "Washington Works." They also made frequent visits to the US to promote

Above *Knife by Samuel C. Wragg, Sheffield, England (c1830s–1860s)*

Right *Joseph Elliot, Sheffield, champagne pattern, all metal.*

Below *"I*XL," George Wostenholm, Sheffield, four-blade shadow senator, genuine stag handles.*

their wares personally, as well as retaining a US office in New York. The strategy paid off, for in a few years, Wostenholm's "I*XL" had become the best-selling, best-known brand in the US, and was sold by every hardware and cutlery merchant. However, the company was ultimately devastated by the application of US tariff laws in 1891, and thereafter only sold a few of its "I*XL" knives in the US to loyal customers. Today, the company's primary outlet is Canada's Hudson Bay Trading Co.

• Joseph Rodgers & Sons—"Star-Cross"

In the 19th century, the best-known brand of cutlery in the world was Joseph Rodgers & Sons of Sheffield. Their famous "Star-Cross" trademark (a six-pointed star trademark, along with the Maltese cross, were granted to a family member in 1882, hence the name "Star-Cross") may have been the first brand to achieve global recognition, and the company's name was, for a time,

synonymous with the very best. In 1820, John Rodgers won a royal warrant, which allowed the firm to add the royal cypher to its mark, and this further aided its reputation as the best-known pocket cutlery brand throughout the British Empire.

• Rodgers-Wostenholm/Richards-Schrade

In 1971, long-term Sheffield rivals Wostenholm and Rodgers merged to form one company, but this was later absorbed by Richards Bros. (scion of the German Richartz firm and British licensee of the Lohr and Stiehl patents for cheap, mass-produced pocketknives), and finally purchased by Imperial-Schrade in 1977. The company was then moved into the largest, most modern plant in Sheffield, where the SCHRADE-I*XL pocketknives were produced and marketed to American collectors. When the company went into receivership, all the Rodgers and Wolstenholm trademarks were sold to the Eggington Group, a small

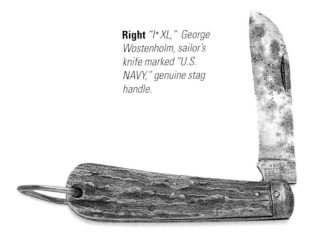

Right *"I* XL," George Wostenholm, sailor's knife marked "U.S. NAVY," genuine stag handle.*

Below *G, Smith & Sons, Sheffield, horseman's knife, with ivory handles; the integral bolster-liners and narrow, square kicks indicate a knife made in Sheffield prior to c1860.*

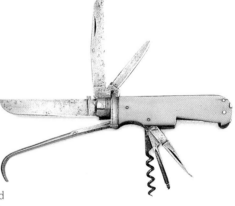

manufacturing firm in Sheffield that produces pocketknives and cutlery for the UK.

While Rodgers and Wostenholm were the English cutlery firms best known outside the UK, other Sheffield-based cutlery firms were equally well known and successful in the British Isles in the 19th century, as follows:

• **Thomas Turner & Company** was founded in 1802, and moved to Norfolk Street in the 1820s. In around 1834, the firm opened its Suffolk Works to make cutlery, tools, and crucible steel. By 1905, Turner was employing roughly 1,000 men, but the firm went out of business in 1932.

• **Mappin Brothers,** which began as the engraving firm of Joseph Mappin in 1810, began to make cutlery in about 1820. In 1851, the firm moved to the Queen's Cutlery Works, where its multiblade sportsman's knives were a specialty, along with several thousand pocketknife patterns. In 1902,

Mappin Bros. was absorbed by an allied firm, Mappin & Webb. Thereafter, the combined firm increasingly specialized in plated wares and jewelry.

• **Unwin & Rodgers** (c1828–1867) was best known for its "patented pistol-knife."

• **Jonathan Crookes & Son** ("Heart-and-Pistol" brand) was founded in 1780. This firm enjoyed a high reputation on both sides of the Atlantic.

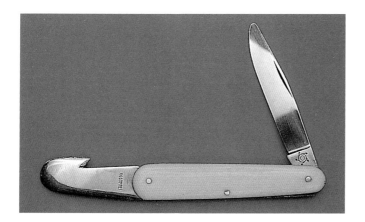

Left *Bone-handled, folding citrus knife by Mueller & Schmidt, Pfeilringwerk (Arrow Circle Works), Solingen.*

• **Brookes & Crookes** ("Atlantic Works") was founded in 1858 by Thomas Crookes and John Brookes, and specialized in elaborate sportsman's and ladies' knives.

• **Harrison Brothers & Howson** enjoyed royal patronage almost from its foundation in 1796 by William Sansom. The firm was acquired in 1847 by James W. Harrison, William Howson, and Henry Harrison, who opened American agencies in New York and San Francisco. Its Alpha Works remained open until 1963.

• **George Ibberson & Co.'s** "Violin"-brand pocketknives, registered in 1880, earned high esteem. The Ibberson family had been prominent in Sheffield cutlery-making since 1666; in 1914, Joseph Ibberson was selected to harden and grind the first stainless-steel knife blades. The firm closed in 1988.

• **George Butler & Co.'s** Trinity Works were founded in 1768. It enjoyed royal patronage, making (among other things) a 600-piece, ivory-handled cutlery set for the Prince of Wales in 1883. Though still in business, Butler's last pocketknives were made in 1972. Butler trademarks included

"Cavendish" (after a noble patron), "Art," and a key logo. Its knives are sold principally in Britain, Australia, India, and other former colonies.

German Brands

Since the late Middle Ages, the city of Solingen, Germany, has been a center of steel and blade manufacture, although it was dependent on the older and larger Cologne for much of its trade. However, a rigid guild structure limited the production of Solingen cutlery for European and world markets. This system was halted when cutlery merchant Peter Daniel Peres was granted a charter by Duke Maximilian of Bavaria to erect the city's first, water-powered pocketknife factory in 1805. Maximilian traded with Napoleon, who abolished all the monopolies and privileges of the Solingen guilds, thus clearing the way for the city's rapid development of its sword-and-cutlery industry.

Solingen's cutlery merchants actively sought to export around the world, and their goods were so competitively priced that even the tariffs could not keep them out of the US market. By 1900, Solingen's

Left *H. Kaufmann & Sons, Solingen, spirit-level knife.*

• SOLINGEN •

These are some of the important Solingen cutlery firms whose pocketknives are now of interest to collectors, with their starting dates (information courtesy Siegfried Rosenkaimer):
Gottlieb Hammesfahr (1684) • Friedrich Herder Abr. Sohn (1727) • J. A. Henckels (1731) • Lauterjung & Son Pumawerk (1769) • Carl Schlieper (1769) • Gebruder Weyersberg (1787) • Peter Daniel Peres (1792) • David Everts (1806) • Peter Daniel Baus (1820) • Alexander Coppel (1821) • Gebruder Christians (1824) • Eduard Wusthof (1832) • Robert Klaas (1834) • C. Lutters & Co. (1840) • Carl & Robert Linder (1842) • Gebruder Krusius (1856) • C. Bertram (1864) • Wilhelm Weltersbach (1882) • Anton Wingen (1888) • Ernst Brueckmann (1891) • Friedrich Olbertz (1915) • Hubertus (1932) •

cutlery exports exceeded those of the US, England, and France combined; virtually every American hardware and cutlery wholesaler offered a selection of low-cost, Solingen-made knives, including a few of the top-quality ones. Unfortunately, World War I closed world markets to German cutlery from 1915 through the 1920s, by which time American firms dominated the cutlery industry. World War II also destroyed much of the Solingen cutlery industry, and although it is still healthy today, it is only a shadow of its former self.

• Heinrich Boker & Co.—"Tree Brand"

In 1837, brothers Hermann and Robert Boker, partners in the sword-making business in Solingen, emigrated to North America. Hermann started H. Boker & Co. in New York City, importing cutlery, tools, and steel from Germany and England, and Robert went to Mexico City, where he founded Casa Roberto Boker. Their cousin, Heinrich Boker, opened a factory in 1869 in

Left *Boker "Tree Brand" muskrat.*

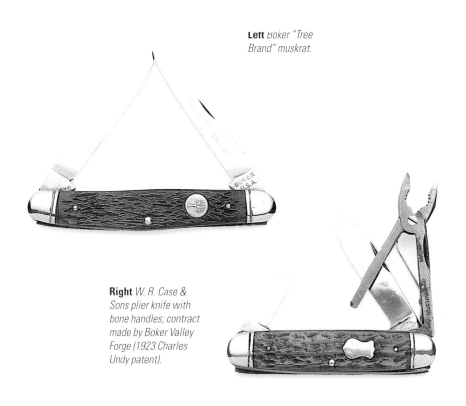

Right *W. R. Case & Sons plier knife with bone handles; contract made by Boker Valley Forge (1923 Charles Undy patent).*

Solingen to manufacture "Tree Brand" pocketknives and cutlery for both brothers to sell; the trademark had been used in the family's tool works in Remscheid. Heinrich also set up his own company in Solingen, and today Heinrich Boker & Co. is a leading private-brand contractor.

• H. Boker & Sons/Valley Forge Cutlery Co.

H. Boker & Sons, like other importers confronted with the US Tariff Act of 1891, sought domestic sources of high-quality pocket cutlery, and in 1899 bought the Valley Forge Cutlery Co. in Newark, New Jersey. Both Boker- and Valley Forge-brand knives were made there, as well as private brands for other distributors, with the Valley Forge brand last being made around 1950. H. Boker & Sons was sold and acquired by various different companies until all US rights to Boker trademarks were resold to Heinrich Boker in Solingen, and Boker's American sales office in Golden, Colorado now sells an up-to-date range of Germany pocket cutlery, amongst other items.

Swiss Cutlery

• Victorinox/Wenger

Victorinox and Wenger are rival firms in
Switzerland that both make red-handled,
multiblade pocketknives for the Swiss army.
Victorinox was created in 1884 by Karl
Elsener, who formed the company's name
by joining his mother's name, Victoria, with
inoxydable, French for "stainless". It is located
in Ibach, and is today owned by Karl
Elsener's descendants. The Wenger firm in
Delemont was established in 1908.

The original "Swiss Army Knife" officer's
model of 1897 was the prototype of all the
commercial versions, a six-blade utility knife
with red, manmade handles. The soldier's
model (1891 to 1960) was a wooden-
handled, three-blade knife with bolsters
including a spear blade and screwdriver at
one end, and a can opener at the other. The
spear blade is often marked with the last
two digits of the year of issue, and since
1961, the soldier's knife has had aluminum
handles, which were also colored red until
1965.

Above *Victorinox "Super Timer," "Classic," and tie pin models.*

FANCY-HANDLED
POCKETKNIVES

I N MOST POCKETKNIVES, the important part is the blade or blades. The blades are the business end, the parts that do the work. There is a class of pocketknife, however, whose principal work is communication rather than cutting. The shape, artwork, and inscriptions on the handles of some pocketknives are more important than the blades, and often it is the handles that do the real work.

Figural Knives

Figural knives are the oldest type. The majority of surviving, ancient-Roman pocketknives are figural knives, whose handles are miniature sculptures of people, parts of the human body (especially legs), animals, or objects.

Advertising Knives

Advertising knives are usually given by business firms as mementos or presents to remind clients and potential customers about the firm, whose name or trademark usually appears on the handle.

Character and Celebrity Knives

Character and celebrity knives depict popular fictional or fantasy characters, or real-life popular heroes—for example, 1880s' pocketknives with cast-pewter handles depicting characters from Gilbert and Sullivan operettas. However, the heyday of character pocketknives was from the late 1930s until the early 1960s, and few are produced today.

The names and faces of political figures appeared on American pocketknives early in the 19th century, and the use of pocketknives in political campaigns continues today.

Perhaps the first entertainment celebrity to endorse the use of his likeness on a pocketknife was William F. "Buffalo Bill" Cody, whose Wild-West show delighted big-city audiences on both sides of the Atlantic.

Photographs of sports heroes have also adorned pocketknife handles since 1910. The first sports star to make an actual endorsement deal for a pocketknife was the legendary baseball player Babe Ruth, in 1930. He received a royalty for allowing his autograph to be reproduced on a baseball-bat figural knife.

Left *Empire Knife Co., West Winsted, CT, silver-handled figural knife.*

Above *Germania Cutlery Works car-design figural knife, imported by Adolph Kastor & Bros., New York, NY.*

Above *Selection of Schrade commemorative knives including (clockwise from top left): Schrade Cutlery's 85th anniversary, 1989; Federal duck-stamp, 1990/1991; US National Park Service 75th anniversary, 1991; 50th anniversary of US entry into World War II, 1991.*

Left *New York Knife Co., Walden, NY, dog figural knife, with carved-pearl handles.*

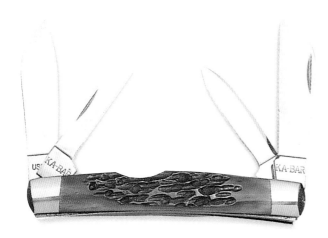

Left *Ka-Bar limited edition congress knife, red stag-bone handles.*

Commemorative Knives

Commemorative knives, inspired by commemorative stamps and coins, record important anniversaries, either public or private. The oldest ones I have seen, commemorating the Battle of Gettysburg, date from 1910, but this type of knife did not become commonplace until the rapid growth of knife collecting after 1970.

Souvenir Knives

Souvenir knives, bought as souvenirs in the location where they were made, are an old tradition. American visitors to Sheffield bought knives as mementos in the 1830s, while visitors to San Francisco in the 1870s bought knives made there by Michael Price or Will & Finck. However, knives made and explicitly marked as souvenirs date back little more than a century. Generally, they are inexpensive, and are designed to appeal to the mass market.

Below *Unmarked aeroplane figural knife.*

Limited-Edition Knives

Limited-edition knives are those made expressly as collector items. Sometimes they are replicas of antique knives, and some are unofficial "commemoratives." Their quality ranges from shoddy to very fine, with the latter always a better bargain than the former, regardless of price.

Of special interest are the limited-edition knife club knives commissioned by local or regional collector clubs, and offered for sale to their members. There are now knife clubs in many places, and they all welcome members who join by mail (see

Above *Annual "Schrade Scrimsaw" wildlife limited-edition set.*

Left *Ambassador (Colonial Knife Co, Providence,RI) miniature keyring knife advertising Greencastle Livestock Market, Greencastle,Pa. "cracked ice" (imitation pearl) celluloid handles.*

Right *Camco (Camillus) "Dick Tracy and Junior" character knife with magnifying glass and whistle.*

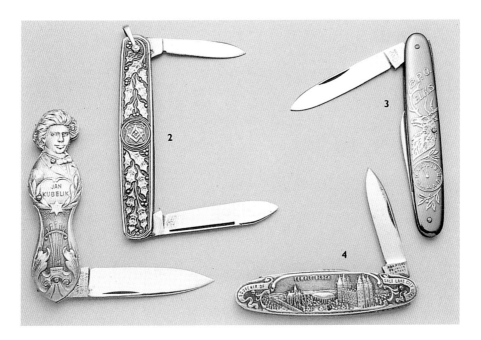

Above *Four fancy, metal-handled knives:*
1. Embossed-pewter figural of Czech violinist Jan Kubelik (1880–1940), by Krusius Brothers, Germany.
2. Embossed-silver senator, Masonic.
3. B.P.O.E. (Elks), etched-and-plated gun metal, made for Coles, New York.
4. A. & A. Mfg. Co. embossed-nickel silver, souvenir of Mormon Temple Block, Salt Lake City, Utah; made in Solingen.

Right *Ambassador (Colonial Knife Co., Providence RI) coin-type knife, advertising Bethlehem, PA Chamber of Commerce.*

Types of Construction

The production technology of fancy-handled knives has evolved over the years. These knives were usually intended for mass-market sale, or to be given away, so low cost was usually a prime consideration. Technological innovations were often applied to advertising and souvenir-knife construction before ordinary pocketknives.

the list in K*nife* W*orld* magazine). Some clubs sponsor knife shows, which draw hundreds of exhibitors and thousands of visitors.

Above *Imperial folding-key knife with Jackmaster sheet celluloid over hollow-steel shell handles advertising Chevrolet cars.*

The list below is a roughly chronological account of the types of handle construction used on fancy knives, along with comments on their application and significance.

• Pressed-Horn Handles

Low-relief scenes were pressed into horn handles using steel dies and steam pressure. These were probably the first mass-produced illustrated handles, and were substantially cheaper to make than earlier figural knives, which were individually handcarved. Individually handcarved figural boxwood handles persisted in Bohemia until World War I.

• Engraved Ivory, Pearl, or Bone Handles

Most of this work, which was still being crafted in the 1930s, was done by hand, and is only found on high-quality advertising knives given to important executives.

• Cast- or Coined-Metal Handles

This technology was rapidly developed during the first year or two of the Civil War (1860–1865). The typical, cheap soldier's jackknife of that period had stamped-brass or cast-iron handles advertising the firm that made the knife. In the 1870s and 1880s, James D. Frary of Bridgeport, Connecticut, made a large business of cheap, pictorial pocketknives with cast-pewter handles. In 1886, after aluminum had become available commercially, P. Daniel Peres specialized in commemorative, souvenir, advertising, and political pocketknives with highly detailed, aluminum handles stamped in deep relief. Thereafter, many firms in Germany, France, and the US offered an endless variety of embossed handles in a variety of metals. Beware—most knives with unplated *brass* handles are modern replicas or counterfeits.

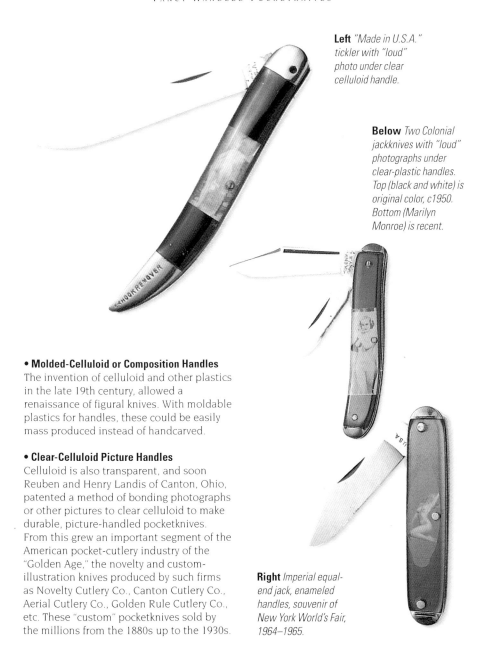

Left *"Made in U.S.A."
tickler with "loud"
photo under clear
celluloid handle.*

Below *Two Colonial
jackknives with "loud"
photographs under
clear-plastic handles.
Top (black and white) is
original color, c1950.
Bottom (Marilyn
Monroe) is recent.*

• **Molded-Celluloid or Composition Handles**
The invention of celluloid and other plastics
in the late 19th century, allowed a
renaissance of figural knives. With moldable
plastics for handles, these could be easily
mass produced instead of handcarved.

• **Clear-Celluloid Picture Handles**
Celluloid is also transparent, and soon
Reuben and Henry Landis of Canton, Ohio,
patented a method of bonding photographs
or other pictures to clear celluloid to make
durable, picture-handled pocketknives.
From this grew an important segment of the
American pocket-cutlery industry of the
"Golden Age," the novelty and custom-
illustration knives produced by such firms
as Novelty Cutlery Co., Canton Cutlery Co.,
Aerial Cutlery Co., Golden Rule Cutlery Co.,
etc. These "custom" pocketknives sold by
the millions from the 1880s up to the 1930s.

Right *Imperial equal-
end jack, enameled
handles, souvenir of
New York World's Fair,
1964–1965.*

Above *Imperial equal-end jack, enameled handles, souvenir of New York World's Fair, 1964–1965.*

• Enameled-Metal Handles

Cloisonné-like enamel-handled pocketknives were developed in Solingen around 1890. Their ornate, gilt-brass frames were filled with multicolored enamels, making a gorgeous effect. Often, these knives, as well as some with engraved-pearl or ivory handles, incorporated tiny Stanhope lens "peepholes," containing miniature photographs (sometimes for advertising, sometimes *risqué*). These knives were very expensive, and their principal consumer was the American brewer, Adolphus Busch, who liked to give them away to people he met on his extensive world travels.

• Color-Etched-Metal Handles

Techniques combining etching with enameling and selective electroplating, developed in Sweden and Germany early in the 20th century, were used to produce a wide variety of pocketknife handles with colorful, attractive, inexpensive, and relatively durable pictures, designs, and advertising messages. These knives are not yet appreciated by collectors as much as they deserve to be.

• Stamped or Lithographed Celluloid and Plastic Handles

These simplest of techniques for decorating handles have been around for over a century, and are today the most widely used. They can vary from a spartan single line of type to elaborate full-color and full-coverage illustrations.

• Metal Inlaid Celluloid or Plastic Handles

The technique of molding silhouettes or words cut from thin sheets of nickel silver into white or imitation-pearl celluloid pocketknife handles was developed in Germany in around 1930. Today, this technique is used on Swiss pocketknives with solid-color plastic handles.

HANDCRAFTED
FOLDING KNIVES

I F YOU HAVE only ever seen pocketknives for sale in hardware, cutlery, or sports shops, you are likely to experience "price-tag shock" the first time you see handmade pocketknives offered for sale at a knife show, art gallery, or jewelry shop. As a rule of thumb, the price of a reasonable, handmade folding knife by a less prominent knifemaker is ten times the price of a factory pocketknife of similar size. A comparable folding knife by a world-renowned maker might cost ten times more. To understand this phenomenon, it helps to have some historical perspective on handmade folding knives.

The "Golden Age"

The half century between 1890 and 1940s was the "Golden Age" of the American pocketknife. Beginning in the 1890s, "protective" tariffs curtailed the access of foreign cutlery firms to the American market. The American firms that had lobbied for higher duties then moved in aggressively to fill the gap. Not only did they take over the US market from their English and German rivals, they also recruited some of the most talented Sheffield and Solingen pocket cutlers.

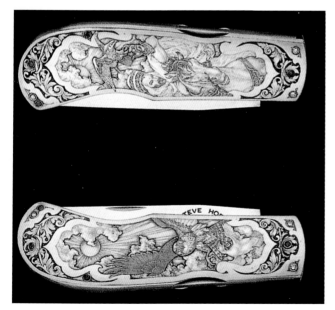

Left and above *"Falconer of the Maghreb." Folding knife by Steve Hoel, 3¼ inches long when closed. Inlaid with gold and engraved by Jon Robyn.*

Right and above *"The Primate Knife." Folding knife by Ron Lake, 3½ inches long closed, with gold-engraved eyeglass screwdriver in the handle. Inlaid with gold and engraved by Ron Smith.*

Above *Schrade LB-7 folding hunter, custom-scrimshaw deer head by Jim Gullette, Greer, SC, 1979.*

Thus reborn, the American pocketknife industry was a conjoining of the best of Old-World handcraftsmanship with the best of American industrial organization, marketing, and innovation. The result, for the American pocketknife buyer, was a rich bounty of wonderful folding knives. This development was interrupted briefly by World War I, but was back on track by 1920.

Before 1940, the best folding knives were in fact handmade. Back then, only a few makers, such as William Scagel and A. C. Cornelison, made small numbers of "indestructible" folding knives by hand.

The "Dark Age"

After World War II, however, the story was different. Many of the important prewar pocketknife manufacturers had left the business, and most remaining pocket cutlery firms had experienced four years of the low standards, limited varieties, and guaranteed profits of war contracts.

During the war, however, while what remained of the cutlery industry was cranking out millions of "adequate" knives,

Left *"Gentleman's Folding Knife" by Ron Lake. Total length when open 4½ inches. 18-carat gold frame and bail, pearl-handle inlays.*

hundreds of individual knifemakers, in and out of uniform, found the opportunity to handmake thousands of better-than-ordinary knives, almost exclusively fixed blades. After the war, demand for handmade knives declined.

The "Renaissance"

The first serious move by an American knifemaker into handmade, folding knives was Al Buck's innovative "Model 110 Folding Hunter" of 1962. Buck never dreamed that this design would revolutionize the folding knife, but it did, opening up a whole new world of markets, both to factory makers and handcrafted-knife makers.

In the early 1970s, a few new craftsmen —including Ron Lake, Bob Hayes, Jess Horn, Jimmy Lile, Paul Poehlmann, Barry Wood, and Robert Ogg—made a solid start that earned them a growing customer following.

Two decades ago, "handmade knife" was virtually synonymous with "fixed-blade knife." There is still some interest today in handmade, fixed blades of the very best quality, but most collectors are interested strictly in handmade folding knives.

Above *"Golden Carp (Koi)." Folding knife by Tim Herman, 3½ inches, closed. Green jade-handle inlays. Gold inlaid and engraved by D. Wilkerson.*

Left *"Wings" folding dagger by Michael Walker. Total length when open 12 inches. Fossilized walrus-ivory handles. Titanium bolsters engraved and toned by Patricia Walker.*

are as well made as the finest Swiss watches, which explains why they are priced in the same range.

Very few of the top folding-knife makers do real "custom" work to customer designs. Some customers have their knives "customized" with fine engraving and/or scrimshaw, but even the most amazing engraving does not enhance resale value *on the knife-collector market.* In the knife-as-jewelry market, however, superb engraving is almost obligatory.

Some handcrafted-knife makers sell directly to customers, but the best way to maximize selection and minimize delay is to buy through dealers who specialize in handmade knives.

Fashions in Folding Knives

Knife collecting is governed by fashions and fads. This is especially true in the collecting of contemporary, handmade knives, because knife makers can, and do, invent new fashions.

A couple of years ago, the hottest area in folding knives was the innovation of blade-locking mechanisms, and new ones were being shown at every knife show. Today, there is still some interest in novel locks, but the most recent trend is simplicity of line and flawless execution.

Another popular area is damascus-steel folding knives. Most damascus is built up of multiple layers of steel, iron, and other metals, up to several thousand layers. When polished and etched, a damascus blade reveals its pattern—sometimes a simple,

Looking at Folding Knives

The most important consideration in handmade folding knives is workmanship: engineering design, materials selection, and the fundamentals of fit and finish. The baseline standard of workmanship—a very high standard—is set by today's factory-made folding knives. Many handcrafted-knife makers cannot equal that standard, so the fact that a knife is made by hand does not necessarily mean it is worth its price. By contrast, the best handmade folding knives

Above *Three views of a "Multalock" folding push-dagger by Ray Appleton. Titanium-handle frame. Note how the complex release button retracts when the blade is in the closed position.*

watered effect, other times with complex patterns or designs.

Exotic metals used for handles and fittings—gold, platinum, and iridium—enjoy a current vogue. Titanium, niobium, and even aluminum, can be toned to bright colors with heat, electricity, and chemicals. Michael and Patricia Walker pioneered this technique on folding knives, along with a much-improved version of the 1906 Cattaraugus "Liner Lock," and attracted many imitators.

An up-coming fashion are "Gentlemen's knives," small, yet exquisite and expensive, hand-made folding knives. Most successful so far have been small jackknives with extra touches such as gold fittings. A few makers have tried penknife and multiblade designs, but many buyers are not ready to spend large sums on little knives, and most makers have not reached the "Golden-Age" level of quality in small knives. I believe that these little, gem-like knives will catch on, partly because of the growing popularity of folding knives, and partly because of their close link to fine jewelry and watches.

A related area is true miniature knives; tiny, perfectly executed, folding knives that are much too small to use. This market is well developed, with many active collectors.

• TODAY'S TOP FOLDING-KNIFE MAKERS •

Here is a list of today's very best, most popular (and most expensive!) folding-knife makers. Expect to pay at least $1,000 for one of their knives.

Apart from this select few, there are several dozen extremely good folding-knife makers, whose work surpasses factory standards. Some of them will undoubtedly join the top rank, as they refine their skills or become better known.

The Ultimate in Basic Folders:
Ron Lake • Steve Hoel • Jess Horn • Dick Hodgson • Warren Osborne • T. R. Overeynder • Jim Corrado • Durvyn Howard • Dwight Towell • W. D. Pease •

Marvelous Mechanisms:
Ray Appleton • Michael Walker •

Dazzling Damascus:
James Schmidt • Jerry Rados • Barry Davis • Stephen Schwarzer •

Right *Two views of "Eagle" folding knife by Harumi Hirayama.*

Embellished by the Makers:
Harumi Hirayama • Michael and Patricia Walker • H. H. Frank • Shiro Furukawa • Tim Herman • Steve Jernigan • Harvey McBurnette •

COUNTERFEITS

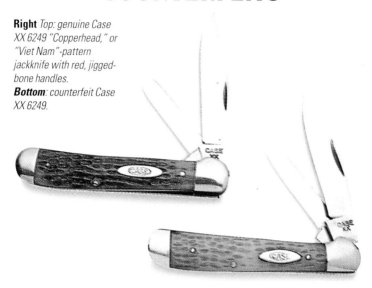

K NIFE COUNTERFEITING FOR the
purpose of cheating collectors began
as a shady "cottage" industry in the 1950s,
with the fabrication of bowie knives. I
noticed them in 1971, but like most
beginners, I learned my first lessons about
counterfeits the hard way, paying good
money for bad knives, but have never made
the *same* mistake twice—however, there are
always new mistakes waiting to be made.

As pocketknives have grown more
popular and more valuable, fakes have
grown more common. Most are still
relatively easy for the experienced collector
to spot, but beginners can be fooled by
slick, shiny fakes. Today at most knife
shows, there are entire tables offering
nothing but fakes; show sponsors have not
yet come up with a satisfactory solution.

Where it Was Made
Can Tell You a Lot

Most fake knives were not made in the same
country as the originals they attempt to copy,
so their materials and construction are
noticeably different from those of the genuine
article. For example, most mass-produced
fakes of older American knives are made in
Germany and Japan, so once you recognize
German and Japanese craftsmanship these
fakes will become obvious to you.

Long before there were knife collectors,
there were already fakes: in the 17th and
18th centuries, Sheffield makers faked
London brands; in the 19th century, German
cutlery firms made up English-sounding
names to put on knives they sold in

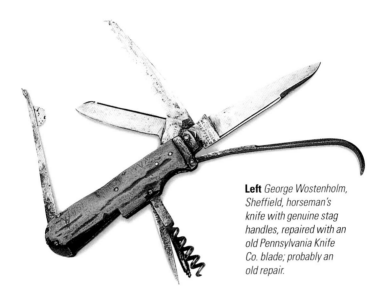

Left *George Wostenholm, Sheffield, horseman's knife with genuine stag handles, repaired with an old Pennsylvania Knife Co. blade; probably an old repair.*

America; while cutlers in India did the same. Today, Germans make fake American knives for American companies, Italians make fake German knives for German *and* American companies, and North Africans make fake Italian knives for their own consumption, because they are cheaper than the real thing. Spaniards make fake French knives for local sale, and so do some French firms. The Japanese fake everyone's knives—not on their own initiative, but because since knife distributors in other countries ask them to (the Japanese are happy to oblige). Meanwhile, Pakistani cutlers imitate the Japanese, the Chinese copy everyone, and everyone copies "Swiss Army" knives!

So what is a poor collector or other knife buyer to do? Look at knives, especially genuine knives, and study how they are made. Materials and workmanship are surer guides to where and when a knife was manufactured than markings, which only matter when they are consistent with the rest of the knife.

Types of Fakery

There are three basic types of fake knives: counterfeits, reworks, and fantasies.

• Counterfeits

A counterfeit is a fake knife that was made in conscious imitation of an authentic knife. Most counterfeits are of inferior quality compared to their originals, but beginners who have never seen an original are likely to be fooled by them. Experience is the best insurance against this type of fake. The majority of knife collectors and dealers will happily loan you their experience and examine a knife you are considering.

The threat of really high-quality counterfeits lurks just over the horizon, but so far it has not arrived. Anyone capable of making a counterfeit of a Remington R1306 "Bullet" that is good enough to fool an advanced collector could probably make more money by making a folding knife of that quality marked with his own name.

• Reworks

Reworks are a much more difficult category than counterfeits. A rework is a genuinely old knife that has been "improved" in some way. The improvement may be relatively minor, such as a patched handle crack or a tightened rivet, but may be a major one, such as an insignificant marking being ground away and replaced by a more popular brand. Most restamping is done with modern stamps, and is easy for the experienced collector to spot, since lettering styles have changed over the years. Some fakers have original, old-stamping dies, however, and then the collector must be familiar with a particular brand in order to avoid being fooled. Lazy fakers engrave or etch fake marks, which should not fool anyone—but they do.

A common form of reworking is the replacement of broken blades, springs, handle covers, or other components. There is a fine line between legitimate restoration, one one side, and fraud, on the other. A legitimate restoration usually incorporates correct original parts, and is always revealed by the seller. Fraud is anything less.

• Fantasy Knives

Fantasy knives would be a glorious joke, if it were not that so many collectors get caught out by them. A fantasy knife is dreamed up by a faker, then marked with famous names in an effort to tie it to history. Fantasy knives are never based on real prototypes, so they are not counterfeits, strictly speaking. Most are glaringly anachronistic in shape, materials, construction, or decoration, but the beginner may not realize this. Many fantasy knives would not function as knives, a sure clue that a "knife" is not genuine.

• NAZI POCKETKNIVES •

In the 1930s and 40s, the German Nazi party ordered millions of fancy daggers decorated with party regalia, in many patterns and variations. These daggers are now popular collector items (and widely faked).

One thing the Nazis did not order was fancy pocketknives. Yet, at many knife shows, gun shows, or swap meets, one is sure to see what *looks* like Nazi pocketknives. They have all the right regalia, sometimes even a portrait of Hltler or his "autograph."

These "Nazi" pocketknives are pure fantasies, dreamed up in the 1970s and sold to the swap-meet trade, mainly by Parker Cutlery Co. of Tennessee. They have now been around long enough to start turning up at antiques stores and estate sales, but they are not genuine, and have no value.

Above
Imaginary Nazi fold-up knife, actually made in England and India.

Below *Paul A. Henckels lobster penknife, all metal.*

FURTHER READING

Knife Magazines

La Passion des Couteaux
Geronimo Organisation
24 Avenue du Recteur Poincare
75016 Paris, France

In French. Bi-monthly. Covers knives around the world, with emphasis on France, USA, Germany; includes custom knives, factory knives, and good historical coverage. On newsstands in French-speaking countries.

Knife Magazine
World Photo Press
3-39-2 Nakano, Nakano-ku
Tokyo 164, Japan

In Japanese. Bi-monthly. Extensive coverage of handmade knives from USA and Japan, factory knives from around the world; technical and how-to articles, knife-show coverage in color, some historical coverage.

Blade Magazine
Krause Publications
700 East State Street
Iola WI 54990, USA

Monthly. *Blade* is the largest-circulation knife magazine, and is available on US and some European newsstands. Features handmade knives, knife shows, Knifemakers Guild news, bowies, books, and lots of ads. I write the "Military Blades" column, and frequent feature stories.

Knife World
Knife World Publications
PO Box 3395
Knoxville TN 37927, USA

Monthly. Tabloid format. Features my "Whut Izzit" column, identifying and valuing unusual knives for readers; also old pocketknives, handmade knives, history, interviews, listing of local knife clubs, and a knife-show calendar; also offers very large selection of knife books for sale by mail worldwide. Free sample copy on request.

Knives Illustrated
Y-Visionary, LP
265 S. Anita Drive, Suite 120
Orange CA 92868, USA

Bi-monthly. Focus on handmade knives; also detailed, well-illustrated articles for the do-it-yourself knife maker. On US newsstands. I contribute occasional feature stories.

Tactical Knives
Harris Publications
1115 Broadway
New York NY 10010, USA

Bi-monthly. Focus on factory and hand-made combat and utility knives.

The Cutting Edge
A. G. Russell Co.
1705 North Thompson
Springdale AR 72764, USA

Monthly. Extensive illustrated listings for handmade and factory knives consigned for sale.

Selected Knife Books

Most knife books in print are available on
http://www.knifeworld.com

Knives '98 (18th Annual) etc.
Krause Publications
700 East State Street
Iola WI 54990, USA
Book format. What the telephone directory
is to a city, this annual has been to the
world of knives since 1981. Includes detailed
worldwide listings, plus solid-feature
articles and hundreds of photos.
Indispensable.

Levine's Guide to Knives and Their Values,
Extensively Revised 4th Edition, by Bernard
Levine, 1997. Now the standard
introduction, reference, and price guide on
all types of knives: folding and fixed blade,
old and new, factory and handmade.
Includes a worldwide list of knife dealers
who cater to collectors.

Knifemakers of Old San Francisco, 2nd Edition, by
Bernard Levine, 1998, newly revised.

The Best of Knife World #3, C. Houston Price
(ed.), 1993. More than 80 feature stories
selected from the popular periodical.

The Sheffield Knife Book, by Geoffrey Tweedale,
1996. Big, well researched, handsomely
illustrated (some color) volume by Britain's
leading cutlery historian.

Pen Knives and Other Folding Knives, by Simon
Moore, 1988. A brief but excellent primer by
the most scholarly writer in the field.

The Official Price Guide, Collector Knives (11th
edition), by C. Houston Price, 1996. Fairly
detailed coverage of popular brands,
selectively illustrated (8 pages in color).

International Blade Collectors Association Price
Guide to Antique Knives, Second Edition, by J.
Bruce Voyles, 1995. Includes moderately
detailed coverage of 31 brands, illustrated
with old catalog cuts, limited coverage of
other brands, useful background material
and charts.

International Blade Collectors Association Price Guide to Commemorative Knives, 1960–1990, by J. Bruce Voyles, 1995. Alphabetical listing of hundreds of limited-edition factory knives.

American Premium Guide to Knives & Razors (4th edition), by Jim Sargent, 1995. Extremely detailed coverage of popular brands: Case, Remington, Winchester, Queen, Robeson, Browning, Pal; mainly illustrated with photos (12 pages in color).

600 Scout Knives, by Joseph Richard Kerr, 1997. Photos and detailed descriptions.

New England Cutlery, by Philip Pankiewicz, 1986. "Scrapbook" of history and documentation on dozens of manufacturers in Connecticut, Massachusetts, Rhode Island, Maine, New Hampshire, and Vermont.

Knife Album, by Robert Mayes, 1970. A large bound volume of old catalog reprints.

The Case Knife Story, by Allen P. Swayne, 1987. Illustrates 75+ Case blade stampings.

Silver Folding Fruit Knives, by Bill Karsten, 1986. Excellent monograph by a leading collector.

U.S. Military Knives, Bayonets & Machetes, Book III and Book IV by M. H. Cole, 1979 and 1990 (all material from out-of-print Books I & II is in Book III). Detailed extensive coverage, mainly using superb line drawings, of both standard and unusual military knives.

United States Military Knives, Collector's Guide, by Michael Silvey and Gary Boyd, 1989. Not as thorough as Cole, but illustrated with photos.

The Knife Collection of Albert Blevins, by Bernard Levine, 1988. Background and inventory of a million-dollar plus collection of handmade knives, including the three dozen now in the Smithsonian's National Museum of American History. Color photos.

La Navaja Espanola Antigua, by Rafael Martinez Del Peral Forton, 1995. Spanish clasp knives. In Spanish.

Knife Collector Organizations

National Knife Collectors Association
(NKCA) (nonprofit)
PO Box 21070
Chattanooga, TN 37424
USA
Operates the National Knife Museum
7201 Shallowford Rd
Chattanooga
Tennessee 37421
USA

There are more than 50 non-profit state and regional knife collector clubs in the United States. Many of them sponsor knife shows and swap-meets, and most of them offer annual limited-edition club knives. For an up-to-date list of knife clubs, knife shows, and knife books for sale by mail, write for a FREE sample copy of KNIFE WORLD magazine: KW Publications, PO Box 3395, Knoxville, TN 37927, USA.

Canadian Knife Collectors Club
Route 1
Milton
Ontario L9T 2X5
Canada

Australasian Knife Collectors
PO Box 268
Morley
WA 6062
Australia

Knifemakers Guild
7148 West Country Gables Drive
Peoria
AZ 85381
USA
A collector may become an Honorary Member for $10 US per year.

MUSEUMS
COLLECTIONS

Note: In all but the specialized knife museums, the knives are generally not on public display. Prior arrangements must be made to view the collections in storage.

The City Museum, Sheffield
Weston Park, Sheffield S10 2TP, England

Victoria and Albert Museum
Cromwell Road, South Kensington
London SW7 2RL, England

German Blade Museum
Klosterhof 4
42653 Solingen-Grafrath, Germany

Solingen Industry Museum
Merscheider Strasse 289
D-42699 Solingen, Germany

Maison des Couteliers
58, rue de la Coutellerie
63300 Thiers, France

National Knife Museum
PO Box 21070, Chattanooga
TN 37424, USA

American Military Edged Weaponry Museum
3562 Old Philadelphia Pike
PO Box 6, Intercourse, PA 17534, USA

Smithsonian Institution
National Museum of American History
1000 Jefferson Drive South West
Washington, DC 20560, USA

Metropolitan Museum of Art
5th Avenue, 82nd Street
New York, NY 10028, USA

California Academy of Sciences
Golden Gate Park
San Francisco, CA 94118, USA

The Oakland Museum
1000 Oak Street, Oakland
CA 94607, USA

Randall Made Knives
4857 South Orange Blossom Trail
Orlando, FL 32839, USA

National Metal Museum
374 Metal Museum Drive
Memphis, TN 38106, USA

The Peabody Essex Museum
East India Square, Salem
MA 01970-3783, USA

Museum of the Fur Trade
6321 Highway 20
Chadron, NE 69337, USA

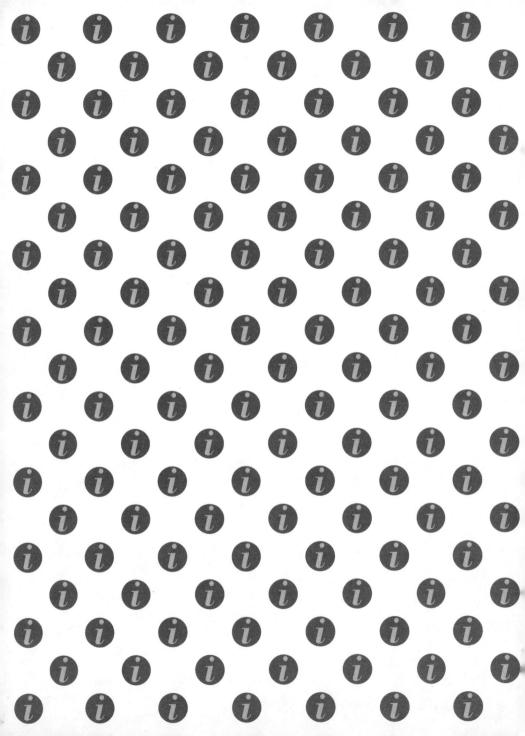